Leckie
the education publisher
for Scotland

Higher
DESIGN AND MANUFACTURE

Course Notes

Richard Knox, Kirsty McDermid,
Stuart McGougan and Scott Urquhart

001/23032020

10 9 8 7 6 5 4 3

ISBN 9780008384418

Published by
Leckie
An imprint of HarperCollins Publishers
Westerhill Road, Bishopbriggs, Glasgow,
G64 2QT
T: 0844 576 8126   F: 0844 576 8131
leckiescotland@harpercollins.co.uk
www.leckiescotland.co.uk

HarperCollins Publishers
Macken House, 39/40 Mayor Street Upper, Dublin 1
D01 C9W8 Ireland

Publisher: Sarah Mitchell
Project Manager: Gillian Bowman

Special thanks to
Jess White (proofread)
Jouve (layout)

The authors would like to thank: Nathan, Nancy, Lisa, Edie, Calum, Stefanie and Evie for their support over the years it took to write this book. Morgen, Molly and Shea for their encouragement and Ruby for lending a hand. Jim for checking and spotting the deliberate mistakes. Anna for her help in pulling this together.

Printed by Ashford Colour Press Ltd

A CIP Catalogue record for this book is available from the British Library.

Acknowledgements

P14 © Keith Homan / Shutterstock.com; P25a © G. Jackson / Getty Images; P25c © Phrontis / CC-BY-SA-3.0; P30a © Catarina Belova / Shutterstock.com; P30b © foto76 / Shutterstock.com; P32a © Fabio Imhoff / Shutterstock; P38c © Thomas Trutschel / Getty Images; P44b © Bloomicon /
Shutterstock.com; P45a © saknakorn / Shutterstock; P4 © HeinzTeh / Shutterstock; P45c © Sorbis / Shutterstoc P45d © charnsitr / Shutterstock; P52 KITEMARK and the I Kitemark device are reproduced with kind permission of T British Standards Institution. They are registered tradema in the United Kingdom and in certain other countries; P5 © Darren Brode / Shutterstock.com; P63 © B.O'Kane / Alan Stock Photo; P64 © David J. Green / Alamy Stock Pho P71a © Bloomberg / Getty Images; P71c © Chris Godda / Creative Commons Attribution-ShareAlike 1.0; P72 Vacclav / Shutterstock.com; P72h © lev radin / Shutterstoc com; P105 © Author team; P106 © nixki / Shutterstoc com; P115 © Author team; P116 © Author team; P146 Author team; P148 ©Author team; P149 © Author tea P150 © Author team; P157 ©Author team; P158 © Auth team; P159 © Author team; P160 © Author team; P161 Author team; P165 © Author team; P166 © Author tear P167 © Author team; P170 © Author team; P171 © Auth team; P174 © Author team; P178 © Author team; P1 © Author team; P181b © Simon Eugster / CC BY-SA 3. P194b © kevin brine / Shutterstock.com; P194c © kev brine / Shutterstock.com; P214 © Author team; P217 Jord – © landmarkmedia / Shutterstock.com; P217 Nike Rose Carson / Shutterstock.com; P217 Lineker – © Mr Pi / Shutterstock.com; P217 Ora – © Mr Pics / Shutterstoc com; P217 Armstrong – © Brad Camembert / Shutterstoc com; P217 Clooney – © Brad Camembert / Shutterstoc com; P218 Puma logo – © tanuha2001 / Shutterstock.con P218 Fowler – © David W. Leindecker / Shutterstock.con P218 Thompson – © BUGNUT23 / Shutterstock.com; P21 Arsenal – © BUGNUT23 / Shutterstock.com; P218 Bo – © Miguel Fernandes / Shutterstock.com; P218 Rihanr –© Debby Wong / Shutterstock.com; P218 Advertisir – © Tooykrub / Shutterstock.com; P218 Packaging – Bloomberg / Getty Images; P218 Website – © Gil C Shutterstock.com;   P219a © Niloo / Shutterstock.con P219d © Justin Sullivan / Getty Images; P227 All image © Festo AG & Co. KG. All rights reserved; P248 SPO Welding, image 3 – © Irina Borsuchenko / Shutterstock.con

Drawings and sketches © Richard Knox, Kirsty McDermic Stuart McGougan and Scott Urquhart

All other images © Shutterstock.com

CONTENTS

Course overview

Assessment Elements

There are two elements to the Course Assessment: the Assignment and the Question Paper. The Course Assessment is graded A–D. There are 170 marks available in total.

The Assignment

The Assignment assesses the application of the skills and knowledge that are gained throughout the Course. A proposal must be generated to address one of the design problems set by SQA. Ninety marks are available for the Assignment. Marks are awarded in the eleven areas shown in the table below.

Activity	Mark range
Carrying out research into a given brief	5
Producing a specification	3
Generating initial ideas	8
Exploring ideas	12
Refining ideas	6
Applying knowledge and understanding of material and assembly processes	10
Applying knowledge and understanding of design issues	12
Applying graphic techniques	12
Demonstrating practical modelling skills	8
Producing a plan for commercial manufacture	6
Applying modelling techniques	8

The Assignment is undertaken over an extended period (under supervised conditions) and the evidence must be presented on twelve A3 pages or equivalent. This includes four proforma sheets issued by the SQA.

1 Carrying out research into a given brief

You are required to carry out research into one of the briefs supplied by the SQA. You should research given issues and any others which you think are important to the task. Your research must be relevant to your chosen brief and generate information which can be included in your specification. You should research issues given within the brief, and any others you identify as important for your task. These may include answering questions on areas such as aesthetics, function, ergonomics, performance and cost. This research should be presented on the proforma issued by the SQA.

You must use primary and secondary research methods (see pages 58–69).

2 Producing a specification

You are required to produce a specification using the information you gained from your research. Your specification, presented on the SQA proforma, should cover a range of issues and have enough detail to help you develop a proposal (see pages 54–55). You may also include key points from the brief in your specification.

3 Generating initial ideas

You are required to generate a range of alternative ideas throughout the design process that demonstrate creativity and address the needs of the problem or situation. Ideas can be generated at any stage of the design process, but they are almost certain to appear at the start of your work, in the form of initial ideas. At this stage you should focus on producing a large quantity of quick ideas rather than a low number of detailed ideas. This will give you a wider base to start your exploration and refinement. You may choose to use idea generation techniques to help with the creation or the development of ideas (see pages 70–79).

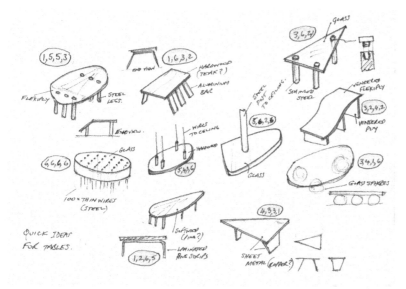

After you have generated initial ideas you are required to develop a design proposal (see pages 86–87) by exploring and refining your initial ideas. This is a particularly important stage as effective exploration and refinement demonstrate your use of modelling and graphic skills, and knowledge and understanding of materials, processes and design issues.

4 Exploring ideas

You are required to explore (see pages 81–83) by considering a range of alternatives. You should use your specification to help you explore, considering alternatives for a range of features. Your exploration should significantly advance your ideas, not make simple superficial changes.

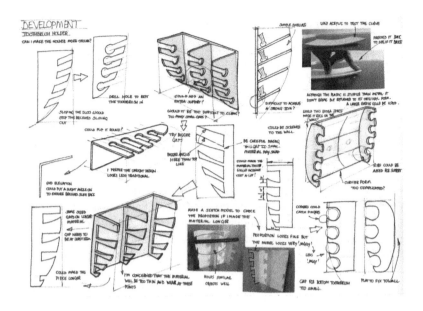

5 Refining ideas

You are required to refine ideas (see pages 84–85) in order to produce a detailed proposal suitable for manufacture. You should refine a range of features of the proposal such as function, sizes, materials, aesthetics and assembly.

6 Applying knowledge and understanding of materials and assembly processes

You have to apply knowledge and understanding of materials and processes (see Section 2) during the development of the proposal. Your knowledge and understanding must be used to advance your solution; simply listing facts about materials and processes will not attract marks. You must apply your knowledge with an aim to detailing appropriate materials, how your components will be manufactured and assembled.

7 Applying knowledge and understanding of design issues

You have to apply knowledge and understanding of design issues (see Section 1) during the development of the proposal. Your knowledge and understanding must be used to advance your solution; simply listing facts about design issues will not attract marks. Good use of the brief and specification provides opportunity to apply knowledge about a range of issues.

8 Applying graphic techniques

You have to apply a range of different graphic techniques appropriate to their purpose of informing and communicating design decisions. You should remember that the graphics have to communicate appropriate detail and information as you develop your solution (see pages 90–102). The quality and type of graphic will vary depending on its use.

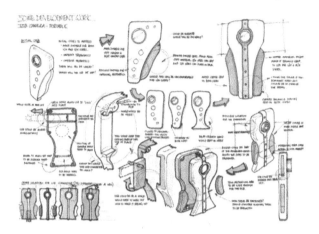

9 Demonstrating practical modelling skills

You have to demonstrate your practical skills (see pages 111–116) through models you have used to develop or communicate aspects of your proposal. The models may be in a range of materials. Your evidence must be presented on the SQA proforma in the form of photographs which demonstrate detail and accuracy.

10 Producing a plan for commercial manufacture

You are required to produce a plan, using the SQA proforma, which details the commercial manufacture for your proposal. Your plan should include: details of component parts (which may be in the form of dimensioned drawings, sketches or photographs of models), details of assembly and a completed product part table.

11 Applying modelling techniques

You have to apply modelling techniques to inform and communicate design decisions. The models must be used to help generate, explore, refine or communicate aspects of the design as you work towards a proposal. The purpose of the models must be clear. See pages 103 – 116.

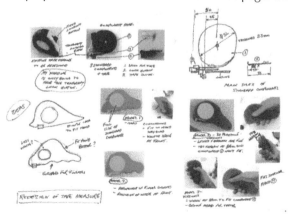

The Question Paper

The Question Paper assesses your ability to retain and integrate knowledge and understanding from across the Course. Eighty marks are available for the Question Paper. The paper consists of two sections, Section 1 and Section 2.

Section 1 features a single question worth 25 marks. The question will be based on the design and manufacture of two similar products. The question focuses on design factors and the justification of materials and manufacturing processes used in their commercial manufacture. It follows a similar format each year and will require extended and reasoned responses.

Section 2 features six or seven questions worth a total of 55 marks. Questions will focus on the design and manufacture of commercial products and the impact design and manufacturing technologies have on society, the environment and the world of work.

Preparing for the Question Paper

The Question Paper is made up of questions from three topics. Each topic has a maximum and minimum amount of marks that can be allocated to it in any one Question Paper. These mark allocations are spread over Section 1 and Section 2 of the Question Paper. The table below shows the topics and their mark range.

Topic	Mark range
Design	30–50
Materials and manufacture	26–42
Impact of design and manufacturing technologies on society, the environment and the world of work	4–8

Design

In this topic you may be tested on:

- your knowledge of the different stages of the design process, such as research, specifications, idea generation and evaluation
- your ability to describe a range of research, idea generation, modelling and graphic techniques that may be used at each stage of the design process and give an example of them in use
- your understanding of the advantages and disadvantages of these different techniques
- your knowledge of the role and impact of the different members of the design team and how they communicate with each other
- your knowledge of the application of communication techniques, including graphics and modelling, the advantages and disadvantages of different methods in different situations and stages of the design process

- your understanding of the factors that influence design, such as ergonomics, function, market, aesthetics and cost
- your understanding of how a given factor may have influenced the design of a specific product
- your understanding of market research, research techniques and their impact on product success
- your understanding of marketing and the advantages and disadvantages of different strategies
- your understanding of branding and its impact on the success of a commercial product.

Note: in this kind of question it is important to be specific, describing the details of the product you have been asked about (shown in the Question Paper) and not to give generic answers.

Materials and manufacturing

In this topic you may be tested on:

- your knowledge of plastics, composites, metals, woods, timber derivatives and their properties
- your knowledge of the impact material selection has on the design, production and function of a product
- your ability to choose suitable materials, with correct reasoning, for a given product or component
- your ability to select materials, with correct reasoning, to suit a given manufacturing process
- your knowledge of commercial manufacturing processes suitable for wood, metal, plastics and composites
- your ability to identify or select, with correct reasoning, commercial manufacturing or assembly processes to suit a given component or product.

Note: you will not be required to describe how any of the commercial manufacturing processes work. You will be assessed on your understanding of the capabilities and limitations of processes and any identifying features left on the manufactured products.

Impact of design and manufacturing technologies on society, the environment and the world of work

In this topic you may be tested on:

- your knowledge of how a designer's decisions and technology influence the impact a product has on the environment and society
- your knowledge of how manufacturing decisions and technology influence the impact a product has on the environment and society.

Literacy skills and command words

By the time you sit the Question Paper you should have acquired the knowledge to answer the questions. You must also have developed the literacy skills to allow you to answer the different styles of questions correctly.

The questions in the Higher paper require you to give an extended response.

In this section you will become familiar with the different types of questions and gain an understanding of the different command words and how to approach them. Command words are used to differentiate the level of response required. The command words you are likely to see in the Question Paper are explained on the following pages.

State and justify

When asked to state, you must give a short factual answer. Alternatives could include: name, identify, give or list. At Higher, state may form the start of the question, so you may be asked to *state* then *justify* your answer.

Example:

Question: *State* an evaluation method that could be used to assess the function of a new vacuum cleaner and *justify* why this evaluation method would be suitable.

Answer: A user trip is a suitable evaluation method. A user trip is suitable because it allows the designer to interact with the product as they would during typical daily use. They would be able to report on any difficulties they experienced with the vacuum, such as awkward switches or ability to lift or dispose of dirt.

Describe

When asked to describe, imagine you are giving instructions or details to someone on the phone. Your aim is to help them visualise in their mind exactly what you can see. More information is needed than a list. When describing you must provide specific details of characteristics and/or features and facts. You might consider 'who, what, where, when and how' to help detail your answer.

Example:

Question: *Describe* how this evaluation method would be used to evaluate the new vacuum cleaner.

Answer: First the designer would plan the best way to carry out the user trip. This would involve vacuuming a range of surfaces, around different obstacles and testing the machine's ability to vacuum up different types of dirt. The designer would then carry out the user trip, starting with selecting the appropriate tool and switching the vacuum on. They would record their observations on performance, noting any difficulties, which they could then use to further improve the next model.

Explain

When asked to explain, you should respond with facts and reasons. First, think about 'why' then consider the events or details that impact the situation and make the relationships between things clear.

Example:

Question: *Explain* why this method is useful for the designer when evaluating the new vacuum cleaner.

Answer: The user trip is useful because it allows the designer to experience the pros and cons of the product first hand. The designer will be able to quickly gain an informed opinion, based on their experience during the user trip. The designer can focus their observations and comments to suit the development needs of the product as they are not relying on vague or mixed responses from members of the public.

Example answers

This section will show you both good and bad examples of responses to exam-style questions from two candidates: Candidate A and Candidate B. Read the questions, then the answers of each candidate. Try to decide if they have understood the command words in the question and successfully written the answer. A summary of their success is illustrated in the table shown opposite.

Questions and Answers

Q1: This product is targeted at adult users. Justify the choice of aesthetics for this market.

Candidate A: The fan is made from a kind of steel, meaning it is silver in colour. The base is round and harmonises with the circular fan shape.

Candidate B: The fan looks like it has been manufactured from steel. This is more suitable for an adult desk or office as it looks more professional and sophisticated than a brightly coloured plastic desk fan. The silver colour will also go with a wide range of interiors. The stand looks similar to a lamp base, so it may be easy for the users to find other products to match. The design is uncomplicated, so most adults will be able to operate it.

Q2: Describe how safety has influenced the design of the fan.

Candidate A: Safety has influenced the design as the fan has a protective cage around the blades to protect the user. The base has been made wide to ensure stability, limiting risk to the user and surrounding area. There is sufficient distance between the back of the fan cage and the handle/ stand to ensure the user can transport the fan safely while it is on.

Candidate B: Safety is all about how well the product meets British Standards. This fan will meet those. The curved corners make the product safe, as does the power switch and the stand.

Q3: Modelling is an important part of the design process. Explain how modelling could have been useful to the designer during the development of the fan.

Candidate A: Modelling can be done in lots of materials and at different stages in the design process. It helps designers generate and test their ideas.

Candidate B: Modelling would have been useful to the designer in lots of ways. A working model would have allowed them to test out the blade design and work out the diameter and depth of the protective cage. A block model could have been used to refine the details of the stand, considering balance, proportion in relation to the other components, and position of and access to the switch.

	Candidate A	Candidate B
Q1	This is not a justification. This candidate simply states some facts about the lamp but they do not give any reasons WHY the designer made these decisions. ✗	This is a good answer. The candidate has made statements and given reasons for them. ✓
Q2	This is a good answer. The candidate clearly describes aspects of the fan and these may have been influenced by safety. ✓	This answer does not communicate any understanding and lacks any description of aspects of the fan. ✗
Q3	This candidate has not answered the question. They have stated some generic facts about modelling and, although these are true, they have not explained how modelling may have been useful during the development of the fan. ✗	This is a good example of an explanation. They have stated the types of models that could be used and given reasons for how these models would have been useful to the designer when developing the fan. ✓

Unit overview

In addition to the Course award, it is possible to gain Unit awards in Design and Manufacture.

There are two Units in the Higher Design and Manufacture Course: **Unit 1 – Design** and **Unit 2 – Materials and Manufacturing**. Each of the Units has two Outcomes, which are further broken down into Assessment Standards.

To gain the Higher Course award you must pass the Assessment for both Units, as well as the Course Assessment.

Unit 1 – Design

This Unit focuses on developing knowledge, understanding and skills in design. In particular, knowledge, understanding and skills will be developed in:

- analysing problems
- using research techniques
- analysing and presenting results of research
- producing detailed and valid specifications
- generating ideas
- using a range of graphic techniques
- using modelling techniques
- exploring design concepts
- refining design concepts
- evaluating design decisions.

Unit 2 – Materials and Manufacturing

This Unit focuses on developing knowledge, understanding and skills in commercial manufacture. In particular, knowledge, understanding and skills will be developed in:

- analysing the materials, manufacture and assembly of a commercial product
- considering the impact of manufacturing processes and production methods on the environment and society
- producing detailed and accurate scale models or prototypes
- using a model or prototype to plan the production of a commercial product
- selecting and justifying materials for the commercial manufacture of products
- selecting and justifying manufacturing and assembly techniques and processes for the commercial manufacture of products.

Unit 1: Design

Outcome 1: Analyse a design brief and produce a detailed specification

To pass the Assessment Standards in this Outcome, you are required to carry out valid research and use your findings to produce a detailed specification. Initially, this involves analysing a brief to identify relevant issues to research.

After planning and carrying out appropriate research, you need to analyse your results and draw conclusions. These conclusions must be used to produce a detailed specification.

Outcome 2: Develop and communicate a proposal to meet a design specification

To pass the Assessment Standards in this Outcome, you are required to apply your knowledge of design and commercial manufacture, and skills in graphics and modelling, to explore and refine a solution to a design task. When exploring, simple changes like rounding corners or changing shape are not sufficient to merit a pass at Higher. Instead you must aim to explore valid aspects that will come from the specification, such as functional requirements, ergonomic constraints or number of components. You will need to evaluate your development decisions against a specification that may be generated from a previous task or given to you by your teacher. This outcome will give you the opportunity to demonstrate your knowledge of design and commercial manufacturing.

You also need to demonstrate your ability to generate a wide range of creative ideas.

When exploring and refining your designs, you are expected to use graphics and modelling appropriately. Graphics and models must always serve a purpose, for example communicating something new or helping you to make development decisions.

Detailed information on these Outcomes can be found on the pages listed:

- Research pages 58–65
- Displaying results pages 66–68
- Specifications pages 54–55
- Evaluation pages 56–57
- Idea generation pages 70–79

Unit 2: Materials and Manufacturing

Outcome 1: Analyse the production of a commercial product

To pass the Assessment Standards in this Outcome, you are required to consider the materials and manufacturing processes used in a product and its sustainability and environmental impact. Your teacher may provide you with a product to analyse. Note that simply describing or stating how the product has been manufactured will not merit a pass. You must consider 'what, why and how':

- What processes, materials and joining methods have been used?
- What alternative processes, materials and joining methods could have been used?
- Why are these materials, processes and assembly methods the best options?
- How sustainable is the product and how does it impact on the environment?

Outcome 2: Plan the production of a commercial product

To pass the Assessment Standards in this Outcome, you are required to produce a detailed prototype or scale model in order to plan the commercial production of a product.

You may plan the production of a commercial product as part of a design activity or your teacher may provide you with an outline of a product.

The model or prototype that you make must have enough detail to allow you to make decisions relating to the manufacture.

Example 1: If planning the manufacture of a tape measure, you are likely to make decisions on the position of split lines, bosses, wall thicknesses, position and depth of screws, etc.

Example 2: If planning the commercial manufacture of a stool, you are likely to make decisions on the final position of components for assembly, details of any jigs, fixtures or formers, economical use of materials, etc.

The model you produce must be an accurate representation of the final product.

You must clearly communicate that the decisions you have made are based on the model. Manufacturing details such as the dimensions of materials, processes and finishes must be clear. Simply listing the processes or assembly methods used will not be sufficient to merit a pass. You must consider the details required for designing parts for manufacture.

Detailed information on these Outcomes can be found on the pages listed:

- Materials pages 122–123
- Manufacturing processes pages 138–139
- Assembly methods pages 176–181
- Planning and production systems pages 184–191

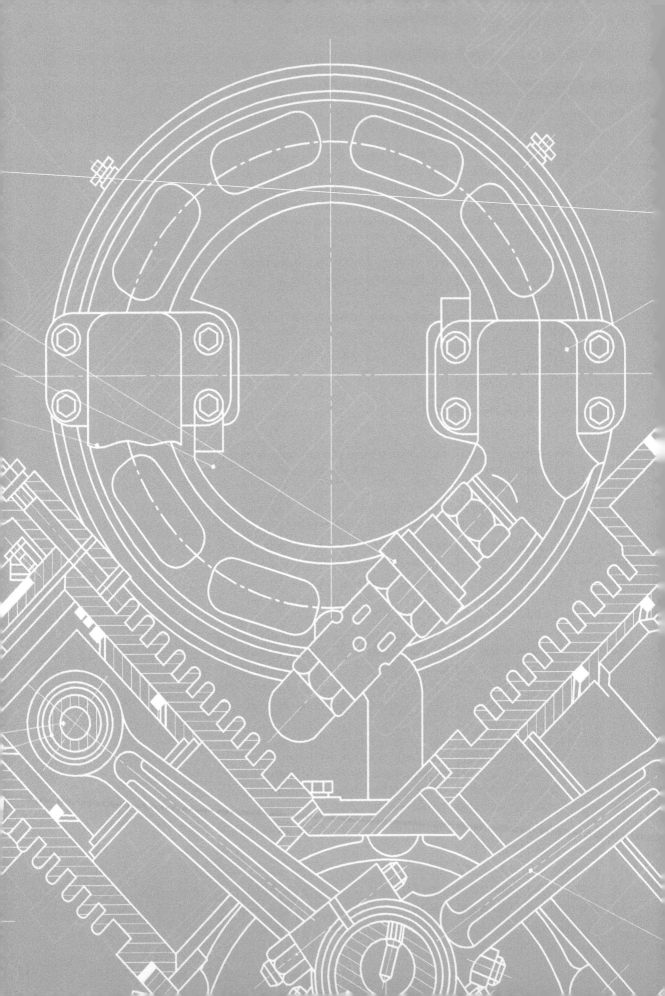

SECTION 1:
Design

1. People who influence design

Products today are seldom designed from start to finish by one person. More often than not a range of people are involved, sometimes organised into teams, each with a different role and responsibility.

By bringing together different specialists, companies are able to develop better products that are less likely to fail in the marketplace.

The main influencers in the design of products are shown in the table below.

Influencer	Role
Designer	Provides the initial inspiration and creative input for the product and, in more recent times, manages the product development.
Market researcher	Conducts market research and provides feedback to the designer on the needs and wants of the consumer. They can also provide feedback to other members of the team on the views of the consumer in relation to pricing, trends and projected sales numbers.
Accountant	Monitors the costs during all stages of the design process. May set caps on spending during various stages to ensure that the product can be produced and marketed at a cost the public is willing to pay. Overspending during research and development (R & D) can have a huge knock-on effect on the final retail price.
Engineer	Tests the various aspects of the product's function. There is a growing number of different types of engineers: structural, electrical, chemical and software engineers all play a part in ensuring products function safely and correctly.
Manufacturer	Ensures the products can be manufactured, provides information on how a product best be manufactured and offers advice to the design team as to how a product may need to be altered to allow it to be manufactured economically and efficiently.
Lawyer	Ensures all legal aspects of a product's design, production, marketing and retail comply with the legislation of the country of sale. They also help make sure that the intellectual property of the design is adequately protected and that the product does not infringe the intellectual property of others.
Materials technologist	Provides information on all aspects of materials, from their properties to the manufacturing methods that can be used. They work closely with the designer, production specialists and manufacturers to ensure the product will perform well and can be manufactured.
Production specialist	Provides information on all aspects of a product's production, from the rate and volume of production to the best production system. They work closely with the designer, materials technologists and manufacturers to ensure the product will perform well and can be manufactured.
Marketing team	Develops the marketing strategies that are used to promote the product. They use the information provided by the market researchers to help publicise the product effectively and often focus on the 3 Ps: price, promotion and product.
Ergonomist	Provides information on all aspects of ergonomics: anthropometrics, physiology and psychology. They use information on gender and age range provided by market researchers to help make the data they provide specific to the intended target market.

Influeuncer	Role
Consumer	Provides feedback (through the market researchers) to the designers, marketing teams and ergonomists on all aspects of the product. Their feedback is vital at all stages of the product development, from its initial inception through to the aftersales experience.
Retailer	Provides feedback, not only on sales rates, but also on what is likely to sell or not. Experienced retailers can give an insight into how successful a product is likely to be, based on models produced prior to full production.
Economist	Monitors market trends and predicts how strong the economy will be by the time the product reaches the marketplace. They work closely with the accountants to make sure that the final product will be economically viable.
Sub-contractor	Provides expertise and services in a range of different fields. They work closely with materials technologists, production specialists, engineers and accountants to ensure the product is manufactured as efficiently as possible. The manufacture of most products relies on sub-contractors at some stage in the design and manufacture.

Skill builder 1.1: The personnel

When the people who influence designs are brought together to form teams, it is important that each member understands their role in the process and what they should contribute to the process.

In pairs or in groups, select and match up the roles and responsibilities of the main design influencers.

Scan for a set of cards showing roles and responsibilities

Example answers on page 204

Skill builder 1.2: Lines of communication

It is important that clear communication takes place between the influencers.

Create a diagram to show the communication connections between the design influencers.

Example answers on page 205

Balancing the roles

For products to be successful in the marketplace, it is important that all those involved in the design play their part and contribute effectively to the final product. Failing to do this will result in products that are likely to be unsuccessful.

The people who influence design can be split into three groups, based on the role they have to play in the design of products.

- Creative thinkers are involved in the development of the product, from the initial concept through to the marketing strategy used to promote it.
- Technical specialists are involved in aspects of the product's material selection and manufacture.
- Business specialists are concerned with the commercial, economic and marketing aspects of the product.

Creative	Technical	Business
Designer Marketing team Ergonomist	Engineer Manufacturer Materials technologist Production specialist Sub-contractor	Market researcher Accountant Lawyer Economist Retailer Consumer

Depending on the type of product being produced, the required inputs from each group will differ.

When all members play their part, there is a balance of creative, technical and business thinking, resulting in a product that is likely to be a success.

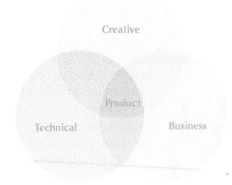

Skill builder 1.3: Balancing the roles

A range of inputs is required if a design is to be successful. If the balance between inputs is skewed towards any one particular area, there is an increased risk of product failure.

Creative, technical and business input is likely to be required if a product is to be successful (refer to selling products pages 42–47). Describe the impact of the balances shown below.

Example answers on page 206

23

2. Function

At the heart of every product's design, there is a fundamental task or purpose that it should carry out; this is called the function. Consumer law states that any item sold must be fit for purpose so, for example, if a kettle is designed to boil water then it must do that. To be functional and fit for purpose, filling and pouring must be safe operations. If a product cannot carry out its intended function for any reason, it is deemed not fit for purpose. The Sale of Goods Act 1979 protects consumers, providing them with the right to return products that are not fit for purpose to the retailer in exchange for a refund.

How to ensure a functional design

In order to ensure a newly designed product is functional, it is important to evaluate the product in full. This goes beyond considering what the product is designed to do, and must take into account the needs of the user and the various ways in which the user might use the product. There is always more than one way to carry out a task. If a product cannot be operated or understood by the intended user, it will not be considered functional.

CASE STUDY

The product

First and foremost, the designer must understand the purpose of the product.

The buggies shown here both carry out the primary function of transporting young children. They both have additional features and functions that appeal to users' needs. One has a rain hood and a storage basket and the other folds up to be very compact. These products, like many others, are often put to use in a range of ways that was not intended. For example some users may hang shopping bags from the handles or use the buggy as a mobile high chair, when out and about.

It is important for the designer to consider how the product will be used, could be used and could be misused.

The design may look good and the product may be operational but the designer must be sure the user will be able to operate it to carry out the desired task. This means fully understanding the target market, their lifestyle and needs, the extent of their experience and difficulties with products and user interfaces. A designer can enhance usability through the semantics of a product. Product semantics are generally visual cues that indicate to the user how to interact with the product.

These visual clues can be achieved using aesthetic elements such as materials, texture, form and colours.

Form follows function

The phrase 'Form follows function' is most commonly associated with the modernist architecture and design of the early 20th century; form being the aesthetic characteristics and function being the operational use of the product. Work from the Bauhaus illustrates this design principle as the function of a design was prioritised, then later enhanced by the aesthetic elements.

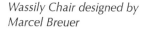

Function word bank

- Primary function
- Secondary function
- Purpose
- Operation
- Use
- Misuse

Wassily Chair designed by Marcel Breuer

Teapot

Skill builder 2.1: Form follows function

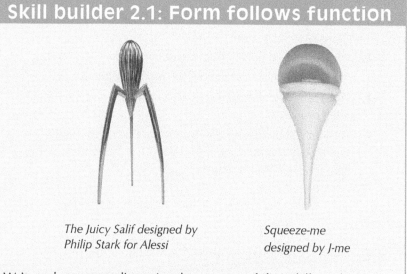

The Juicy Salif designed by Philip Stark for Alessi

Squeeze-me designed by J-me

Write a short report discussing the concept of 'form follows function' for two products that have been designed with a similar function in mind, like the lemon squeezers shown above.

In your report you should refer to:

- functional aspects of the products
- balance of function and aesthetics.

Example answers on page 207

How will the user know the product is working?

For certain products it is important for the product to provide the user with some kind of feedback that lets them know the product is carrying out its function. Building in feedback, from sound or visual indicators, will alter the user's experience of the product. Although this feedback function is really part of the product's ergonomics, it reassures the user of the product's performance, satisfying their needs and encouraging them to reuse the product.

Skill builder 2.2: Functional analysis

Carry out a functional analysis of a small domestic product like the anglepoise lamp shown above.

1. What is the function or purpose of the product?
2. Describe in simple terms how the product operates.
3. What features or components are visible that aid the function of the product?
4. Consider in basic terms the input, processes and output required for the product to function fully. Show these using a diagram like the one below.

Input ⟶ Process ⟶ Output

5. What do you not know about the function of the product?

Example answers on page 207

Products are always designed with an intended purpose and method of operation. Being familiar with their product, the designer may find it easy to operate but will the users? The designer can carry out evaluations (pages 56–57) when developing the design to ensure the product is functional and useable by the intended market. Bear in mind that consumers will not always use the product as it was intended. They may find additional and unintentional uses for the product, which could potentially cause harm to the user or to the product itself.

Skill builder 2.3: Consumer use

The chair shown above is functional and fit for purpose.

1. Describe how the product is intended to be used.

2. Other than the intended use, list more ways in which a user might use (secondary functions) or misuse the product.

3. Consider how the product might respond to the identified intended and unintended use and misuse.

4. Redesign the chair with additional functions that may increase the appeal of the product. You should do this through a series of quick annotated sketches.

Example answers on page 208

3. Aesthetics

Aesthetics is the human perception of beauty, including sight, smell, sound, touch, taste and movement. It is more than just how things look.

A product's aesthetics can alter the user's experience and perception of a product in several ways, some of which will be subconscious.

Designers can use aesthetics to make products more attractive, safer and easier to use. Designers, therefore, need to have an understanding of the elements that affect aesthetics, how to apply them and the impact they have on consumer perceptions.

How do people develop aesthetic senses?

A baby is a blank canvas as far as their preferences for aesthetics are concerned. As they begin to grow and develop they naturally find themselves being drawn to things that they find attractive and pleasing such as the look, feel or sound of a favourite toy or the taste or smell of a favourite food. These early aesthetic preferences are based on emotional responses.

Even in the early years, our preferences for particular aesthetics allow us to communicate aspects of our identity, style and personality that are rooted in our social and emotional needs.

Consider the occasion of being bought something to wear that you find nothing short of embarrassing. It is unlikely the buyer intended to embarrass you. It may be that their perception was that the product was good value, well made or practical, whereas your concerns are more likely to be about colour, style or how you will feel wearing the item.

As people grow older and gain more experience of the world and the products around them, their appreciation and understanding of design matures and they begin to consider aesthetics on a deeper level. Aesthetics may influence perception of other aspects of the product such as:

- Does it appear to be easy to use?
- Does it feel as though it is good quality?
- Is it good value?
- Does it appear to be safe?

 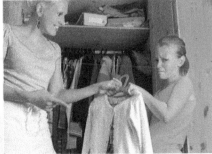

Application of aesthetics in design

In today's global market, aesthetics can be used to distinguish products from others in the market. Changing aesthetic elements, like materials and texture, will impact other design factors, and vice versa.

It is important that the designer creates the correct aesthetic to appeal to the target market. They can check this by carrying out market research. In order to be effective, market research must address the appropriate aesthetic elements.

Skill builder 3.1 provides you with an aesthetic vocabulary and an opportunity to demonstrate and develop your understanding of these terms.

Skill builder 3.1: Using aesthetic vocabulary

Some of the terms used to describe aesthetics are given in the table. If you don't know the meaning of any of these words, research them before starting this task.

The rooms below have some aesthetic similarities, but evoke different emotional responses. Use the appropriate aesthetic terms to compare and describe the characteristics of the two rooms.

Visual	Sound	Tactile	Smell	Taste
Colour	Pitch	Texture	Strength	Texture
Shape/Form	Tone	Weight	Bitter	Bitter
Line	Volume	Comfort	Sweet	Sweet
Symmetry	Repetition	Temperature	Sour	Sour
Pattern	Quality	Form	Pleasantness	Pleasantness
Proportion		Quality		Strength
Balance				
Materials				

Compare the impact of the aesthetics for the users of the two rooms.

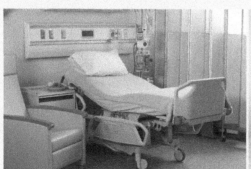 

Example answers on page 209

Skill builder 3.2: Comparing aesthetics

Evaluating the aesthetic characteristics of products will develop your understanding of how design decisions alter the appearance and our perception of products.

Compare the aesthetic appeal of the Fiat 500s shown below.

How have the aesthetics evolved over time? Use the aesthetic terms in the table on page 27 to help. You should think about all aesthetic elements that are relevant. Consider the different reasons why both cars are appealing today.

Example answers on page 209

Skill builder 3.3: Aesthetic product analysis

Analyse the aesthetic characteristics of a product such as:

- an iron
- a hairdryer
- a kettle.

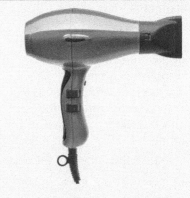

Use a series of quick annotated sketches or photographs to illustrate how the aesthetics of the product impact the:

- function of the product
- ergonomics of the product.

Refer to function on pages 24–27 and ergonomics on pages 32–41.

Example answers on pages 210–211

The following skill builders require you to be creative. It is unlikely that your results will match the suggested answer in this book. The key to these tasks is understanding how altering the product's aesthetics impacts other aspects of the design and the user's perception of the product.

Skill builder 3.4: Other factors impact on aesthetics

Any change we make to a design will alter the product's aesthetics in some way. Make changes to the toaster shown below that will:

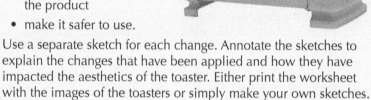

- improve the function by making the toast easier to remove
- make it easier to clean
- make it easier to manufacture
- increase the stability of the product
- make it safer to use.

Use a separate sketch for each change. Annotate the sketches to explain the changes that have been applied and how they have impacted the aesthetics of the toaster. Either print the worksheet with the images of the toasters or simply make your own sketches.

Example answers on page 212

Skill builder 3.5: Making aesthetic changes

When changing the aesthetics of a design, you will probably impact other aspects of the product. This task helps you identify the knock-on effects of aesthetic changes.

You can use the printable worksheets or plain paper.

Develop the following design by applying the following aesthetic changes:

- alter the shape
- alter the proportion
- add two elements of contrast
- use symmetry
- use line
- add pattern
- alter the form
- alter the visual balance.

Consider how the aesthetic changes have altered other aspects of the design, such as function.

Example answers on page 212

Scan for aesthetics worksheets

4. Ergonomics

The study of ergonomics aims to improve interactions between people and their products or environment by making tasks easier, less frustrating, more comfortable and safer to carry out.

The importance of ergonomics

During the 1900s there were various 'scientific management' studies, which looked at increasing the efficiency and productivity of workers by improving the ergonomics of the task. For example, Frank and Lillian Gilbreth's 'Time and Motion' study looked at different techniques that would reduce the amount of unnecessary motions required to perform a task. One study into bricklaying improved productivity from laying 120 to 350 bricks per hour.

It wasn't until the 1940s that ergonomics emerged as a scientific discipline. During World War II, technical equipment for the military was becoming increasingly complex to use. High cognitive demands were made of the user and there was a realisation that optimal results would not be achieved if the user found it difficult to understand or use the equipment.

This was particularly true with the design of aircraft cockpits. Extensive studies were carried out by a group of **physiologists** and **psychologists** who analysed the interaction between pilot and plane with an aim to ensure:

- the control-panel layout was easy to understand
- all controls were within easy reach of all pilots
- maximum comfort, especially for longer flights
- controls were easy to operate with reasonable strength and effort from the pilots
- the effects of vibration and noise were minimised.

Although initial studies focused on the work environment, ergonomics is now widely recognised and essential for the good design of commercially produced products for domestic and specialist fields.

Identifying how ergonomics impact design

In general terms, a product that has been designed with ergonomics in mind will be safe, easy and comfortable to use.

🔍 CASE STUDY

Ergonomics of a vacuum cleaner

Consider how ergonomics would impact the design of a vacuum cleaner.

- A vacuum cleaner should be comfortable to use by a range of users.
- The height should adjust to suit a range of users. The handle size should allow big and small hands to hold it comfortably. The noise from the vacuum should be tolerable.
- Buttons and switches should be easy to press with fingers and/or feet.
- There should be easy access to the buttons and switches. They should operate with reasonable force or effort.
- The attachments should be easy to store, remove from their positions, fit and use.
- The required action should be clear and the force and effort required should be within reasonable limits. There should be adequate clearance for access. Colours and textures can be used to help identify, remove, fit and use functional parts.
- The user needs to know when to empty the vacuum; there should be a visual, audio or other cue.
- The user needs to know when the vacuum is turned on or off; there should be a visual, audio or other cue.
- The user should be able to use the vacuum without injury or strain.
- The weight of the vacuum should be reasonable for someone of normal strength, so that the user can push and pull it without too much effort. The height must be suitable to avoid arm and back strain. The vacuum should be easy to turn and manoeuvre with minimal strain or effort.

Ergonomic word bank

- Reach
- Clearance
- Strength
- Force
- Effort
- Sound
- Smell
- Texture
- Taste
- Vibration
- Movement
- Size
- Grip
- Weight
- Response
- Proximity
- Fatigue
- Strain
- Safety

Skill builder 4.1: Ergonomics for good design

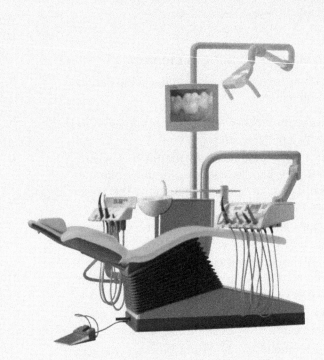

The dental chair above is designed with two different users in mind; the dentist and the patient.

Consider what is required to ensure a dental chair is safe, easy and comfortable to use from the dentist's point of view.

Think about your own experience at the dentist. Consider what is required to ensure a dental chair is safe, easy and comfortable to use for the patient.

Analyse the dental chair using the same method as the vacuum cleaner example, detailing how ergonomics could impact the design of the dental chair for the dentist and the patient.

Use the ergonomic word bank on the left to help you complete this Skill builder.

Example answers on page 213

Ergonomics is a huge area of study that is commonly broken down into three distinct areas: anthropometrics, physiology and psychology. The vacuum cleaner case study and the skill builder above have already touched on all of these areas. It is important that you understand the significance of each of the three aspects of ergonomics, how they have influenced the design of commercial products, and how you can apply them during design tasks.

Understanding the aspects of ergonomics and good design

A product with good ergonomic design should be **intuitive to use**. If a user feels confused, unsure or stressed by any aspect of the product, this will have a negative impact on their experience. The way a product looks, feels, sounds, smells and even tastes can affect the user's perception and use of it. These **feelings** and **perceptions** are the powerful **psychological** aspect of ergonomics.

A well-designed product only requires *reasonable* strain or effort from the user. Any product that requires high levels of force to operate will result in user fatigue, strain or injury, especially if used repeatedly or for long periods of time. This does not necessarily mean that everything should require the least effort possible; some products require a certain level of strength to prevent accidental use. Designers always have to consider **how different parts of the human body work** and interact with products; this is the **physiological** aspect of ergonomics.

Knowing and understanding the **physical measurement and limitations** of a person's size and form is essential if a product or space is to have good ergonomic design. Designers should ensure there is sufficient access to, or space between components to allow easy, safe and comfortable use for the full range of intended users. This is the **anthropometric** aspect of ergonomics.

Skill builder 4.2: Different aspects of ergonomics

It is important to make specific connections between an exact part of a product and how the user interacts with it.

Skill builder 4.1 identified how ergonomics can impact design. During the design of the dental chair the designer needs to be familiar with the different areas of ergonomics to understand what data or research should be applied.

Create a list or annotate the worksheets provided, detailing:

- the anthropometric data (specific body sizes and range of movement) that are important for parts of the design
- the physiological considerations that determine the strength or effort required to use the chair
- the psychological impact different aspects of the design may have on either user: the dentist or the patient.

Example answers on page 213

Scan for ergonomics worksheet

Applying ergonomics for a better designed solution: anthropometrics

First, the designer needs to gather **relevant** data to ensure they can accommodate the full range of intended users of the product or space.

Identifying the age, gender and ethnicity of the intended users allows the designer to research the extremes in the range of user sizes. This information is essential to ensure the majority of users have suitable reach, clearance, and range of movement to be able to use the product easily and safely.

Consider designing a shoe locker. The height and size of the unit and individual shoe compartment would change considerably if we were designing it for primary children, a public gym or a professional American male basketball team.

A designer can obtain **anthropometric data** by measuring the relevant sizes of a sample of people, or more likely by using existing information which is available in software or data tables like the one shown at the bottom of the page.

Understanding percentiles

Humans differ in size considerably. When plotted on a graph, the frequency of the range of sizes from smallest to largest result in a distribution which produces a bell curve as shown below.

Any human size such as shoulder with, foot length or standing height, will produce a similar distribution.

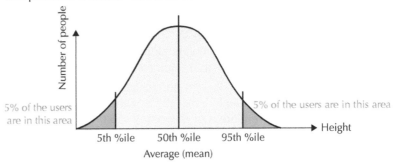

A designer can select data ranging from the first percentile (1ˢᵗ %ile, smallest) to the 100ᵗʰ percentile (largest). The data selection depends on the specific product or space and intended users.

A common mistake can be to design for the 50ᵗʰ percentile, the average size.

The average (50ᵗʰ %ile) shoe size of American male basketball players is UK size 15, whereas the largest (100 %ile) shoe size is 22. Designing the lockers with the 50th percentile data would exclude users in the 51ˢᵗ to 100ᵗʰ percentile as their shoes would be too large to fit.

Gender and ethnicity also affect the selection of appropriate percentiles as illustrated in the data table below.

Data table showing percentile standing height (in mm) of men and women aged 19–65 from the UK, USA and Japan.

	M 5th	M 50th	M 95th	F 5th	F 50th	F 95th
UK	1625	1740	1855	1505	1610	1710
USA	1640	1755	1870	1520	1625	1730
Japan	1560	1655	1750	1450	1530	1610

Anthropometrics class activity

Use two different coloured pens or pieces of chalk; one for the boys and one for the girls. Each person should take a turn to stand in front of the board, arm stretched up and hand facing forward holding the pen or chalk.

Draw a short horizontal line on the board and put your initials next to it.

Once complete, you should see that the standing reach of your classmates varies. The majority will be clustered closer together but there is likely to be one unusually high or very low.

Create a table to record the heights of your classmates in ascending order. Repeat for the boys and the girls, creating three sets of data.

What differences are there in the range of sizes and the average of each data set?

Now consider the maximum height for:

- an emergency stop button that everyone can reach
- a shelf that all the girls can reach
- a shelf that all the boys can reach.

Anthropometric considerations

- Intended users
- Range of sizes
- Data tables
- Appropriate percentiles
- Inclusive design
- Age
- Gender
- Ethnicity
- Situation

Skill builder 4.3: Selecting critical sizes

Designers may make allowances for variables, like outdoor clothing, when selecting appropriate sizes.

With this in mind, use the data table in the appendix on page 200 to select the minimum sizes for the following areas of the children's playground. Justify your selection.

1. Diameter of flume – to fit all children sliding.

2. Width of red slide – up to age 5.

3. Height of red roof up to age 6 – children standing.

4. Height of opening to flume slide – all children sitting.

5. Height of swing frame to allow all adults clearance.

6. Height of swing seat – allow all children to sit safely.

Example answers on page 214

Physiology considerations

- Range of movement
- Type of movement
- Strength
- Effort
- Fatigue or strain
- Physical limitations
- Coordination
- Inclusive design
- Reaction time

Physiology

Physiology is focused upon specific characteristics and mechanisms of the human body such as range of movement, fatigue and strength.

A common mistake is to assume all products should be as light or easy to use as possible.

Consider a medicine bottle. The strength and coordination required for the combination of push, squeeze and turn, is necessary to prevent access from children. If the bottle was too easy to open, young children may be able to open it and drink the contents.

It is easy to take for granted the simple actions we carry out every day, like picking things up, opening a packet, putting a key in a lock or typing a message on a phone. However, not all consumers are equally able bodied, nimble or sharp-sighted.

Ensuring that design is accessible for a range of users, despite their physical limitations, is essential. This means understanding the needs and limitations of the user.

Kraft foods used an arthritis-simulation glove in the development of their easygrip lid for Maxwell House coffee. The glove restricted the wearer's finger strength and movement, allowing a true evaluation of the ease of use of the lid design.

Companies have also developed age-simulation suits like the one shown below. These help able-bodied people understand a wider range of difficulties. As well as being useful for designers, these suits are being used by organisations such as the NHS and Barclays to ensure they cater to the ability of their clients.

Skill builder 4.4: Physiology from a different perspective

Follow the instructions at the bottom of the page to make an arthritis simulation glove.

Carry out the following tasks with and without the gloves, considering the ease and time taken to complete the task in each case. Record the key difficulties people with arthritis may have when carrying out everyday tasks.

Activity	With/ without glove	Time taken	Ease of use	Key difficulties
Pick up a pencil and write the alphabet	without			
	with			
Use a key to unlock a door	without			
	with			
Open a drinks bottle	without			
	with			

Use modelling to design a solution for one of the above problems. Refer to pages 103–116 if you need advice on modelling.

Example answer on page 214

Making arthritis simulation gloves

You will need:

- eighteen two-pence coins per hand
- sticky tape
- two gloves per hand, preferably one rubber glove for the inner glove and one knitted glove to cover. Expanding 'magic' gloves make effective covers.

Directions:

- Put on the rubber gloves. Tape the two-pence coins to the fingers in between the joints as shown. It may be difficult to attach all the coins to small hands.
- Once all the coins are on, cover hands with the knitted gloves.
- You can now carry out tasks experiencing the restricted strength and movement of arthritis sufferers.

Psychology

Psychology is the study of mental processes such as perception and memory. These processes are influenced by how something looks, feels, sounds, smells and tastes. Therefore, it is important to consider psychology when designing products.

Understanding how users behave and react in different situations is important for good user-centred design. This will prevent feelings of failure or frustration when users don't understand how to use a product or system.

User-centred design should make it easy for the user to:

- determine what actions can be carried out
- understand the results of their actual and potential actions
- evaluate the current state of the product
- interact naturally with the product's or system's layout.

Don Norman defined seven stages of action that underpin how a user moves from an **intended action** to **completed task**.

	Step		Example
1	Forming a goal	**What do I want?**	Boiled water
2	Forming the intention	**What would satisfy this goal?**	Using the kettle
3	Specifying an action	**What do I have to do to achieve the intention?**	Fill up the kettle and press the switch to turn it on
4	Executing the action	**Do the steps I have specified**	Filled the kettle and pressed the switch
5	Perceiving the state of the world	**Use my senses to gather information about the world and/or system I am working in**	Do I hear it boiling? Do I see steam? Can I feel the heat?
6	Interpreting the state of the world	**Figure out what, if anything, has changed**	Has the water boiled?
7	Evaluating the outcome	**Did I achieve my goal?**	Yes

The user needs to be able to carry out the intended operation (use the product) with ease. Designers should:

- avoid over complicating products with unnecessary features
- ensure the interface has good semantics (the product is intuitive to use)
- ensure the location of functions and mode of use are clear
- ensure each action is confirmed by feedback from the product
- design to mitigate user error.

Skill builder 4.5: Psychology – seven steps of action

Apply Norman's seven stages of action for the following goals:

- Sending a message on a touch-screen phone.
- Making a piece of toast.

In each case, explain how human senses could be used to enhance the user's experience of using the product.

Example answers on page 215

It is through our senses that we are either attracted to or repelled by products. Our senses can alert us to danger or create a pleasurable user experience.

The position, layout and proximity of functional parts also affects the user's confidence in the product's margin of error and influences their optimum reaction time.

Skill builder 4.6: Psychology

Consider the psychological aspects associated with the two products shown: the external glass lift and the iron.

1. Explain how paying attention to each of the senses could improve the user's experience of these products.

   Try to be specific, relating the senses to functional aspects of the products. Outline how the senses receive feedback during use of the products, leading to the user's perception of their experiences.

2. Give examples of how altering the aesthetic features could be used to alert or deter the user.

3. Explain how proximity and familiarity could be used to improve the user's experience of the products.

Example answers on page 216

Psychology word bank

- Senses
- Perception
- Emotional response
- Awareness
- Recognition
- Product/process feedback
- Semantics

5. Selling products

The starting point for new products often arises due to technology push or market pull.

Technology push

Technology push is when research and development in new technology drives the development of new products. This may be a result of new materials with improved properties or improvements in manufacturing processes may mean a manufacturer can make the product cheaper or more efficiently. Many electronic products, such as mobile phones, have been launched due to technology push.

Market pull

Market pull is when products are produced as a result of market demand. The demand may be generated by such things as consumers wanting new or improved products or by a competing product being launched by another manufacturer.

The market

Commercial products are designed and made to be sold. The market (potential buyers) at which the product is aimed will influence its development and how it is promoted.

Successful products meet consumer needs and often fill a gap in the market. In order to fully understand the consumers' needs, **market research** should be carried out. Market research involves gathering data about potential buyers, competitors and market trends. Accurate market research reduces the risk associated with launching new or improved products. Market research may be carried out using a range of research techniques (see page 58). To generate useful information the market research must be aimed at the correct market, known as the target market.

Target market

A target market is a group of consumers to which a company directs its product(s). Target markets can be further divided using the following aspects:

- **Geographic**: for example, region, size of population, density of population, climate.
- **Demographic**: such as, age, income, occupation, education, household size, and stage in the family life cycle.
- **Psychographic**: for example, attitudes, values, opinions and lifestyles.
- **Behavioural** (relationship to a product): for example, brand loyalty, occasions that stimulate purchases, first time buyer, regular buyer.

Having a well-defined target market is useful when the product is launched as this is the first element in a successful marketing strategy.

Marketing strategy

The aim of a marketing strategy is to match products with the people who need and want them.

When marketing products, companies need to create a successful marketing mix, which is commonly known as the four Ps:

- The right **product**: it must have the right features to appeal to the target market.
- Sold at the right **price**: it must be able to be compete in the market and make a profit.
- In the right **place**: it must in the right place at the right time, for example in a retail store, online or at special events.
- Using a suitable **promotion**: the target group needs to be made aware of the product. This may be done in a number of ways:
  - » advertising through channels such as TV and online, social media, direct mail and publications
  - » sponsorship of events or celebrity endorsement
  - » creative packaging design and point-of-sale materials
  - » special offer promotions.

Marketing is about more than just advertising and sales. It is everything a company does to get customers and keep them. It is also about after-sales activity, such as providing support and dealing with complaints.

Skill builder 5.1: Celebrity endorsement

Companies often use celebrities to endorse their products. Although this can dramatically increase market exposure and sales, it can backfire if the celebrity becomes involved in something that attracts negative publicity.

Carry out research into the use of celebrity endorsement and produce a presentation. The presentation can be in any form you wish and may include the following:

- a range of products that have been endorsed by celebrities
- how much the celebrities received
- details of the impact the endorsement had on sales
- examples whereby a company has 'dropped' a celebrity.

Example answers on page 217

Niche marketing

Niche marketing concentrates all marketing efforts on a small and well-defined segment of the population.

Companies that concentrate on niche segments aim to be successful by being a big fish in a small pond instead of being a small fish in a big pond. Targeting a product at a niche segment has several advantages and disadvantages for a company.

Advantages of niche marketing	Disadvantages
Less competition of production	Can be expensive due to low volumes
Clear focus: easier to target customers	Over-dependence on a single product
Builds up market expertise	Success will attract competition
Customers may pay higher prices and be more loyal	Very vulnerable to market changes

Brands

A brand is much more than simply a name or logo. A brand consists of all the impressions and experiences associated with a company or product.

Branding is the sum of things such as:

- Reputation
- Attitude
- A promise
- Logo
- Products
- Feeling
- Customer service

Consumers can relate to a brand on a rational and on an emotional level and can develop **brand loyalty** when expectations are met. Consumers can have different levels of brand loyalty:

- **Brand recognition**: the consumer knows something about the brand.
- **Brand preference**: the consumer prefers the brand but will buy another if it is not available.
- **Brand insistence**: the consumer will only buy the brand.

Companies try to create a consistent and recognisable image, known as **brand identity**. Elements of brand identity include brand name, logos, tagline and personalised symbols or characters. The elements used to create the brand identity should be used to reinforce brand values every time there is contact or a **touch point** with customers. A touch point can be defined as the way the target market interacts with a company, whether it be person-to-person, through a website, an app or any form of communication.

Skill builder 5.2: Branding

Choose a brand to which you would consider yourself loyal (because you prefer or insist on it). Create an image board showing ways in which the company have built up their brand identity. Add annotations giving information about the touch points where the company reinforced the brand's values.

Example answers on page 218

Product launch

It is very difficult to launch a new product onto the market: in fact, most launches fail! There are numerous reasons for launch failure.

1. Market research

- Little or no market research may have been carried out meaning that the product was developed because the designers 'thought' there was a market for it.
- Poor market research can lead to a poorly defined market and marketing that lacks focus.
- The product may be 'interesting' but lacks a precise target.

2. Finance and distribution

- Most of the budget may have been spent developing the product, leaving little left for the launch.
- Distribution may have been slower than expected, falling too far behind the launch.
- Supplies may be insufficient to meet demand.
- The launch may not match with the key selling season.

3. Differences in an updated product

- The sales force, retailers and target market may not have been educated about the changes to the new product. This results in poor sales.

4. Problems with the product

- There may be issues with quality of the product, perhaps with function or safety, which result in poor feedback.
- The price of the product may be too high.

Unsuccessful product launches can harm a company financially and damage its reputation. The company may be left with unsold stock or, in the event of a design fault or a quality control issue, there may be a product recall. Even the largest of companies have had their share of disastrous launches but most have managed to survive.

Handling a product recall

The impact of a product recall can be minimised if a company handles it well. In fact, a well-handled recall can enhance a company's reputation. The recall procedure will vary depending on type of product but will include the following:

- Everyone (including retailers and distributors) involved with the manufacture and sale of the product should be informed of the impending product recall.
- All customers should be notified of the defect and the procedure for rectifying the problem.
- A recall management team should be set up to deal with recall.
- Production should be suspended if required.
- Quality assurance processes should be updated.

Skill builder 5.3: Product launch failure

Carry out research into failed product launches.

- Create a poster that gives details of a range of product launch failures.

OR

- Produce a presentation about product launch failures to show your classmates.

Example answers on page 219

6. Performance

Maintenance

Maintenance keeps a product working smoothly and safely.

Maintenance will enable the user to:

- keep their product in good working order
- extend the life of the product.

The level of skill required to maintain a product should be considered carefully during the development of a product.

Products that are easy to maintain are less likely to be thrown away, which is of benefit to the environment. However, products that can be maintained indefinitely reduce the potential for repeat purchases, limiting profit for companies.

During the design of a product the designer should consider different aspects of maintenance.

Who is likely to carry out maintenance?

The skill level of the end-user will influence how much maintenance can be designed into the product.

For example, high-end mountain bikes are likely to be purchased by enthusiasts. These users will have a fair degree of skill in repairing and maintaining their bikes, as well as the specialist tools to manage this. Maintenance will include complicated tasks such as servicing the shock absorbers or hydraulic brakes. On a cheaper bike, maintenance might be limited to simple cleaning tasks, the periodic tightening of bolts and repairing punctures.

Regardless of user skill level, it is good practice to design to ensure that any maintenance is as simple as possible to carry out.

What type of maintenance should be carried out?

Consideration must be given to the nature of the maintenance tasks. Will the product need charged, filled, emptied or adjusted? Will parts need replaced? The designer must ensure that access to perform these tasks is included in the design.

Skill builder 6.1: Maintenance issues

Choose a product with which you are familiar and describe the maintenance tasks you would expect to be carried out during its lifespan.

Describe how the designer has made these tasks as simple as possible to carry out.

Example answers on page 220

Value for money

All consumers want value for money. Companies attempt to design and manufacture products that, while similarly priced to their competitors, are perceived as being better value.

To ensure that the perception of 'good value for money' is achieved, the designer must take the expectations of the target market into account.

Designers will research expectations prior to forming a specification (see pages 54–55) and will try to find out, for a given price point:

- what functions the market expects the product to perform
- which performance criteria are most important to the market
- how long the market expects the product to last.

With these points in mind, the designer must strike a balance between fulfilling the consumers' expectations and keeping costs to a minimum.

Consideration must also be given to the selection of materials and the manufacturing processes. These must be affordable enough to allow a profit to be made on the product. At the same time, however, the consumer must believe that the product has been well manufactured from quality material.

In their pursuit to gain the best value for money, consumers will compare similar products against one another. Products that offer that little bit more than their competitors will stand out.

Through the internet and social media, consumers have increasing access to a wide range of product reviews and other users' opinions on the quality or effectiveness of products. When it comes to purchasing new products, consumers are better informed than ever. Ensuring that consumers feel they are getting a good deal is becoming ever more important.

Planned obsolescence

Products are not designed to last indefinitely. There are obvious reasons for this. Designing and manufacturing such products would have significant financial implications in the form of material and manufacturing costs. These products may also be difficult to dispose of and they are also likely to become unfashionable after a while.

Moreover, it is in the best interest of companies to encourage consumers to make repeat purchases of the same product. This increases sales volumes. Companies achieve this by regularly releasing more up-to-date products featuring better technology or designs that are more fashionable.

Planned obsolescence is a strategy used in the design of products to give a product a specific lifespan – to cause the product to be *perceived* as **obsolete** before it actually needs to be replaced. This encourages the consumer to purchase another version of the same product before it is actually needed.

Companies using planned obsolescence must strike a balance between encouraging repeat purchases and maintaining customer loyalty.

Skill builder 6.2: Repeat purchases

Create a list of **five** products you can think of that you have bought more than once. Do not include consumables such as food.

Identify the products you think are designed with planned obsolescence in mind.

Explain why you think this is the case for each identified product.

Example answers on page 220

Planned obsolescence can be achieved in three ways.

Style obsolescence

Products that are designed to be fashionable on their release are likely to fall out of fashion within the next few years. Some products, such as clothing and electronic goods, are more susceptible to this form of obsolescence than others. Designers try to anticipate the time it will take for a product to become unfashionable. Fashion influences issues such as aesthetics and material selection during the design of the product.

Product evolution

The increasing rate of technological developments has resulted in a steady stream of newer models and product upgrades onto the market. For example, consumers have become accustomed to purchasing a new mobile phone or computer every few years.

Companies encourage consumers to make these regular purchases by frequently introducing models with more modern or high-tech features. In doing so, the company can continually generate a *buzz* for its products. This also helps to convince consumers to make repeat purchases. How often have we purchased a product just because it is the latest version and not through any real need for it?

Ease of maintenance

The lifespan of any product is influenced by how easy it is to maintain.

Consider the razors shown to the right. The disposable razors will only be used a few times before being thrown away. It is unlikely that the user will try to sharpen the blades. The more expensive razor has a replaceable head, which will be changed when it is perceived to be blunt. This will ensure that the more expensive razor will have a longer lifespan.

Some mobile phone manufacturers make it very difficult to replace phone batteries. When the battery performance inevitably begins to deteriorate, the consumer, given the hassle and expense of paying for new parts and a repair, is just as likely to purchase a new phone.

Skill builder 6.3: Planned obsolescence

Carry out internet research and explain what is meant by the following:

- throwaway society
- consumerism.

Refer to products with which you are familiar in your answer.

Example answers on page 221

---

7. Safety

Safety is paramount in the design, manufacture, use and disposal of all products. Designers have a key role to play identifying and eliminating potential hazards and reducing possible risks from hazards if elimination is not possible.

Safety during design and development

The designer must consider how the product will be used. This not only involves understanding the product's proper intended use, but also how the product may be misused. Selection of materials, finishes, ergonomic aspects, instructions and the user interface are just some of the aspects the designer may consider in relation to product use. It is also necessary to ensure the product is designed in line with any regulations, such as those set out by the British Standards Institution (BSI). This organisation sets and regulates standards for products and systems. The Conformité Européene (CE) certifies that products meet European standards.

Rigorous testing can be carried out during development. This often involves using machines to test products in extreme environments or to simulate extended use in a shorter period of time. Refer to test rigs on page 63.

Safety during the manufacture

The production should be safe for those involved. There are numerous laws protecting and regulating Health and Safety at work. Manufacturers need to protect their workers from repetitive strain, gasses, fumes, falling objects, factory noise, etc. This can be achieved by maintaining machines, through signage, training, alert systems, regular breaks, adequate lighting and use of personal protective equipment (PPE), such as eye protection, hard hats and gloves.

Safety for consumer use

The product should be easy to understand. Where a risk cannot be eliminated, regulatory warnings such as those shown on the left should be clearly visible to alert the user to any potential risk due to intended use or misuse of the product.

The materials chosen or operation of the product should not cause any harm to the user. Any special requirements relating to the use, maintenance or disposal of parts (such as risk of electrical shock or toxicity of lithium batteries) should be made clear to the consumer.

LIFT CORRECTLY

Safety at end of life

It is the designer's responsibility to consider any risk to society or the environment that may be caused by disposal of the product. The designer must ensure products can be dismantled safely for disposal and that any toxic parts are protected in sealed units to guard against accidental access.

Skill builder 7.1: Safety and the family car

Consider a typical family car.

Explain how safety considerations have influenced the design of the car.

Try to come up with at least 10 less obvious points. For example, one aspect might be the speed at which the windows open and close. A slower speed would prevent the glass from shattering and potentially reduce the risk of people getting fingers caught.

Example answers on page 221

Skill builder 7.2: Identifying hazards and eliminating risk

Consider the product lifecycle shown below.

Select a product of your choice and explain the risks or hazards the product could cause at each stage and how these could be reduced or eliminated.

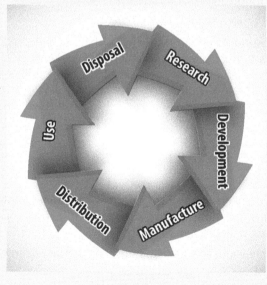

Example answers on page 222

Safety word bank

- Legislation
- Certification
- BSI
- CE
- Testing
- PPE
- Staff training
- Machine maintenance
- Misuse
- Hazard and risk
- Warnings
- Signs and symbols
- Disposal

8. Analysing problems

The first stage in solving any problem is clearly understanding it. This is as true in design and manufacture as in any part of life. Understanding a design and manufacture problem might involve clarifying a brief to draw up a specification or thinking about the best way to evaluate an existing product.

Clarifying a brief

The starting point of the design process is usually a **design brief**. The design brief is normally supplied by a client and should contain an outline of the requirements of the solution.

An **open brief** provides general guidelines and offers the opportunity for a wide range of possible outcomes. A **closed brief** is more specific and detailed in its requirements. This gives the client greater control over the process but can limit the range of possible outcomes.

Whichever type of brief is used, it is important that the designer and client are both clear on what is required of the solution. In order to clarify the brief it has to be analysed, key issues identified and research carried out.

Specifications

A **technical specification** describes what the product does *after* it has been designed.

A **product design specification** (PDS) describes the requirements of the solution, i.e. the PDS is for products that have *not yet been designed*. The details of a PDS vary according to the brief but often contain details of the following:

- **Performance**
  What does the product need to do? What is that key functional data? (What speed, how often, how is it to be powered, what loads will it experience? How long and how often will the product be expected to perform – perhaps twice a day for two minutes for an electric toothbrush, or all through the working day for an office chair.)

  The performance required is likely to impact on materials, assembly methods and the costs of the product.

- **Dimensions**
  Are there restrictions on the product's dimensions, for example size or weight? The restrictions may be expressed as a range between a maximum and a minimum value.

  The product's dimensions are likely to impact on its manufacture, transport and cost.

- **Conditions of use**
  What conditions will the product experience during manufacture, storage, transportation and use? The temperature, humidity, and exposure to dirt, dust, insects, vibration, noise, corrosive fluids or chemicals will all impact on various aspects of the product such as the choice of materials and the manufacturing methods used.

- **Cost**
  How much will the product be expected to retail for? How much will the target market pay? What price are similar products? Material and manufacturing costs are approximately 30% of final retail price.

- **Customers**
  Who is the target market? Their profile (age, lifestyle, social type) will impact on aspects such as retail price, quantity manufactured, ergonomics and aesthetics.

- **Quantity**
  How many units should be produced? This will impact on manufacturing processes and costs.

- **Legal requirements**
  Are there any special standards with which the product must comply? There may be British Standards (BS) to follow.

- **Environmental considerations**
  Are there any environmental restrictions on the product? Consideration should be given to manufacture, use and disposal (or recycling) of the product. This will impact on materials, manufacturing processes and costs.

- **Timescale**
  Are there deadlines for the project? Phase timescales and a project timing overview may be required – see project planning on pages 184–186.

- **Lifespan**
  How long is the product expected to last? Planned obsolescence may need to be considered.

- **Maintenance**
  Is regular maintenance of the product required? This will affect the assembly of the product, accessibility of parts and instructions and special tools may be required.

- **Packaging**
  Is packaging required for the product? Packaging constraints may affect the design of the product and could have environmental implications.

Evaluating products

Product evaluation is carried out for **two** main reasons:

- Existing products are evaluated by designers and manufacturers when developing ideas for new or improved products.
- Products are evaluated during development to ensure they meet the PDS and perform as required.

In everyday life, evaluation of products takes place at a subconscious level. Often, people form instant opinions about products. However, designers and manufacturers need to evaluate more systematically, using criteria against which a balanced judgment can be made.

The first stage in carrying out an evaluation is identifying the criteria to be used. The criteria can be thought of in two main ways: **aspects** of the product or **design factors**. Consider the bike shown (left).

If *aspects* of the product are used to evaluate the bike, the evaluation may include things like:

- The brakes. How well do they work? Can the intended user operate them easily?
- The pedals. Are they a suitable size for the intended user? Are they durable?

If *design factors* are used to evaluate the bike, the evaluation might include things like:

- **Function**
  How well do the brakes work? How easy is it to change gears?

- **Ergonomics**
  Do the user's feet fit on the pedals? Are the brake levers a suitable size for the user's hands?

It can be seen that both approaches may generate similar information about the bike. The use of aspects or design factors depends on the product, the designer's preference and the audience for the product evaluation report.

It is important that the product evaluation provides useful information about the product. To generate useful information you should be clear about why you are doing the evaluation. Lack of clarity will lead to inappropriate research methods and wasted time.

The table opposite compares the evaluations of a hammer and a pair of running shoes, highlighting that different information is required in each case.

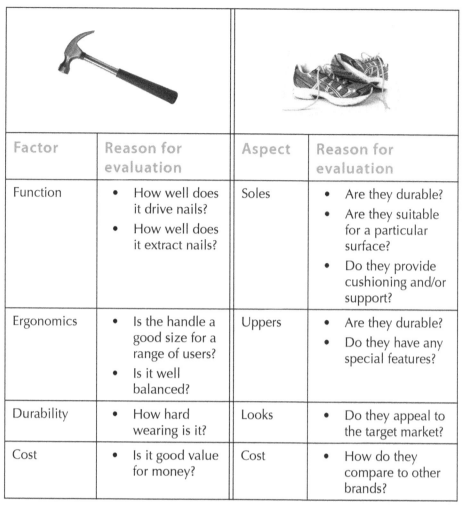

Factor	Reason for evaluation	Aspect	Reason for evaluation
Function	• How well does it drive nails? • How well does it extract nails?	Soles	• Are they durable? • Are they suitable for a particular surface? • Do they provide cushioning and/or support?
Ergonomics	• Is the handle a good size for a range of users? • Is it well balanced?	Uppers	• Are they durable? • Do they have any special features?
Durability	• How hard wearing is it?	Looks	• Do they appeal to the target market?
Cost	• Is it good value for money?	Cost	• How do they compare to other brands?

Skill builder 8.1: Evaluation criteria

List the criteria you would use to evaluate the products shown below. Give reasons for your choice.

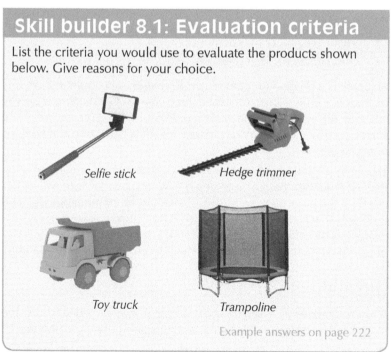

Selfie stick

Hedge trimmer

Toy truck

Trampoline

Example answers on page 222

9. Gathering information

Gathering valid information is a key skill often required in Design and Manufacture. Information can be obtained from primary or secondary sources.

- **Primary source information** is factual and comes from an original, first-hand account, such as the results of a questionnaire.
- **Secondary source information** interprets primary information, for example, someone's analysis of the results of a questionnaire.

Before starting to gather information you have a few questions to think about. What information is required? How will it be gathered? How will it be displayed?

What information is required?

Information may be required for a variety of reasons, for example:

- evaluate existing products
- analyse a design brief
- refine a design proposal
- evaluate a design proposal.

How will information be gathered?

There is a range of methods of gathering information, such as:

- questionnaires
- user trips
- user trials
- test rigs
- use of secondary information
- comparison to other products.

A survey is a process for gathering information that could involve any of the data collection methods named above. Conducting a survey takes in all aspects of the information gathering process including survey construction, methods of sampling, data collection and analysis of information.

The method used to gather data will depend on the type of information that is required. Before you begin any data collection, you must establish the purpose of your investigation, what information you need and decide whether you have selected an appropriate method. For example, you could not draw a valid conclusion regarding the durability of a product just by asking people whether they thought it was durable.

Questionnaire

A questionnaire is a set of questions that can be filled in by the interviewer or by the person being asked the questions (the respondent).

Care must be taken in designing the questionnaire. The following should be considered:

1. Be clear about the information that you require

Consider how the information you gather will be analysed.

2. Decide on who and how many should be questioned

A sample of people should be selected so that a range of opinion is gathered with as little bias as possible. A large sample requires greater time and energy but will provide more reliable information.

3. Decide on how the questionnaire will be completed

- Questionnaires can be presented as written questions on paper or using an online tool, such as SurveyMonkey. The questions are completed or 'filled in' by the participant.

- Face-to-face interviews involve an interviewer asking questions to an individual person.

- Telephone surveys involve an interviewer asking questions verbally to a single, usually anonymous individual on the phone.

4. Draft the questionnaire

Remember to consider the best order of the questions.

Closed questions may be used. These tend to produce data that can be quantified. They can take the form of a question such as 'Do you prefer brand X or brand Y?' or they may ask the respondent to pick a category as shown below.

> How important is it to you that the leisure centre has up-to-date equipment?
>
> Very important ☐
>
> Fairly important ☐
>
> Not important ☐

Respondents may also be allowed to pick more than one category.

> In which of the following countries have you been on holiday in the last five years? Please tick as many as apply to you.
>
> UK ☐
>
> France ☐
>
> Spain ☐
>
> Greece ☐
>
> Other ☐

Respondents may also be asked to rank given answers, such as shown here.

Please rank the following pizza toppings according to this scale: 1 = you like the most, 5 = you like the least.

Pepperoni ☐

Cheese ☐

Chicken ☐

Pineapple ☐

Peppers ☐

Issues may also be ranked using a matrix.

Please rate the following aspects of our service.

	Poor	Fair	Neutral	Good	Excellent
The speed of service	O	O	O	O	O
The quality of food	O	O	O	O	O
The quality of drink	O	O	O	O	O

Open-ended questions may also be used. These allow the respondent freedom to formulate a reply in their own words. Normally, there will be one or more blank lines provided for this purpose. Open-ended questions can be used in the following situations:

- When it is not clear what the response is likely to be, for example, 'Why did you decide to select brand X?'
- When the possible responses are too many to list.
- To allow a respondent to explain their response to a preceding closed question.
- To avoid pre-judging answers.
- To obtain quotes that can enliven a report.

Open-ended questions can generate a wide range of answers, which can be difficult to analyse.

5. Test the questionnaire

Try out your questionnaire with friends and family or a 'pilot' group. There may be questions that:

- have a different meaning to that which was intended
- cannot be understood
- are too difficult to answer
- do not discriminate between respondents, so that everyone gives the same answer
- lead the respondent to an inappropriate part of the questionnaire.

If a respondent cannot answer a question for any of these reasons, they may become 'stranded' and not complete the process.

Any problem questions should be edited before the questionnaire goes 'live'.

6. Distribute and collect the questionnaire

Tasks include:

- writing the covering letter to accompany the questionnaire
- providing details about how, where and when to return the questionnaire
- setting a due date for the return of questionnaires (ensure that the date allows a reasonable amount of time for people to complete and return the questionnaire, but not so long as to allow them to misplace it)
- organising a method and place of return.

7. Analyse and display the results

An analysis is necessary to make sense of the data collected. It is important to consider how the data will be analysed when designing the questionnaire.

Sorting and tallying of responses to closed questions can be done by hand. An advantage of online questionnaires is that sorting and tallying of responses can be done by the program, eliminating any arithmetic errors.

Data from closed questions is often displayed in charts or graphs, generated using spreadsheet programs. Another advantage of online questionnaires is that they can automatically generate charts and graphs of the information.

Analysis of open-ended questions is more complex. When discussing the results from open-ended questions, it is better to generalise about the frequency of responses, for example 'the majority…', 'most respondents indicated…'.

User trip

A user trip is a good method of finding out how well a product works. This type of evaluation can be carried out on an existing product or on a prototype of a design proposal. A user trip involves going through the process of using the product.

Carrying out a user trip can help identify any problems with a product and can be used to compare products. A user trip that identifies a problem with a product can lead to a design opportunity.

A few things should be considered before the user trip is carried out.

- **The conditions under which the user trip will be carried out.** There are a number of variables that may have an impact on the results; the user trip could be undertaken at different times of the day or in different locations.
- **The method of recording results.** Notes may be taken by the person carrying out the trip or by an observer. Photographs or video may be used to record the user trip.

User trial

In user trials a product is tested by 'real users' in a relatively controlled or experimental setting, where they are given a standardised set of tasks to perform. The result can be a 'problem list', which contains valuable information regarding the potential for improving the usability of a product.

User trials are normally used to evaluate existing products but are often used on pre-production prototypes to identify any issues. Data can be gathered by observing the user trying out the product as they talk through their interactions with the product and by making notes about any problems they experienced.

This can be supplemented by a more formal set of questions asked after the trial has been completed.

Test rigs

Test rigs are used to perform physical tests on products. Test rigs are often used to check prototypes as they can repeat many actions over a short period of time to simulate extended use of the product.

Rigs can be constructed to test a wide range of features of products, for example chairs can be tested using specially designed rigs, shown here.

Bending test rig for seat and back rests

Skill builder 9.1: Test rigs

Carry out research into test rigs and produce a report on how a product of your choice is tested using rigs.

A useful starting point may be www.satra.co.uk

Example answers on page 223

Use of secondary information

Secondary information may be gathered from a range of sources, such as:

- books, magazines, newspaper
- TV and radio
- the internet.

It is important that any possible bias in the original source of the information is considered when analysing the information. For example, if the information was gained from the manufacturer's website, it is very unlikely to be negative about the product!

Comparison to other products

Information on a product is often gathered by comparing it to other similar products.

People often compare products before they buy them, so that they can get the 'best buy'. They may compare the product to other similar products, look at and touch it or ask for their friends' opinions if they already have the product.

People can also consult commercially available independent reviews. These include *Which* magazine, which carries out evaluations on a wide range of products. 'Which' reports are now also available online at a cost.

There is a range of websites which give comparisons of products in specialist areas, for example *http://runrepeat.com/compare-running-shoes* compares a wide range of running shoes and presents information in the form of a table.

Designers often compare products to try to improve them or to identify a market opportunity.

The aspects compared will depend on the product. These may be physical aspects of the product or particular components of the product, for example the effectiveness of the brakes of a bike or the comfort of the seat of the bike.

Design issues such as aesthetics or ergonomics can also be compared. The aspects chosen for comparison should be appropriate to the intended use of the product – there is little value in comparing the lifespan of a disposable razor.

The information gathered from comparisons is often displayed in a table.

Note that product comparison tables generally list comparisons of the technical features of products rather than areas such as aesthetics or ease of use.

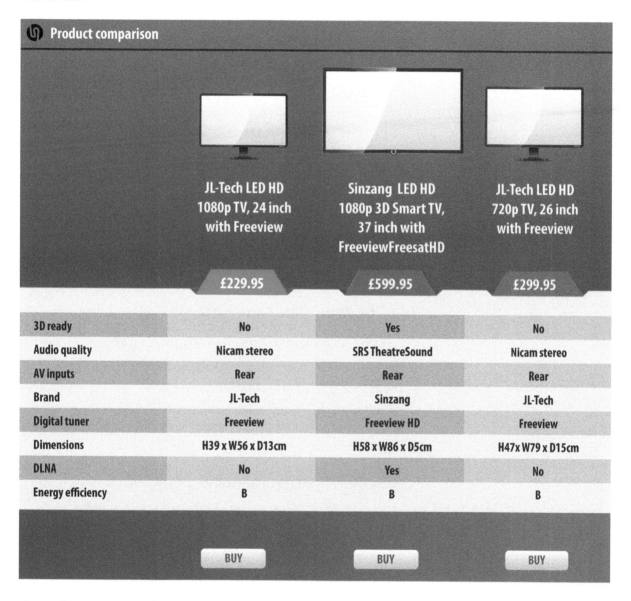

Product comparison	JL-Tech LED HD 1080p TV, 24 inch with Freeview	Sinzang LED HD 1080p 3D Smart TV, 37 inch with FreeviewFreesatHD	JL-Tech LED HD 720p TV, 26 inch with Freeview
	£229.95	£599.95	£299.95
3D ready	No	Yes	No
Audio quality	Nicam stereo	SRS TheatreSound	Nicam stereo
AV inputs	Rear	Rear	Rear
Brand	JL-Tech	Sinzang	JL-Tech
Digital tuner	Freeview	Freeview HD	Freeview
Dimensions	H39 x W56 x D13cm	H58 x W86 x D5cm	H47x W79 x D15cm
DLNA	No	Yes	No
Energy efficiency	B	B	B
	BUY	BUY	BUY

Listing the comparative features of products is a fairly straightforward task. However, the contents of the list must be analysed and conclusions drawn for the information to be of any value.

Displaying information

After you have gathered information it is important to analyse it and to display the results clearly and effectively. Your research will have generated a lot of 'raw' data that must be put into a manageable form so that you, and possibly others, such as a client, can make sense of it. The way you organise and display your data will depend on the type of data you've gathered.

- If you have conducted an open-ended questionnaire, you'll need to look for patterns and trends in the responses. You must be careful with the use of this type of information. It can be difficult to draw conclusions. For example, if a few respondents make similar comments about a product you cannot conclude that this is a general opinion.

- If your research has generated numerical data, you can summarise and display the data using graphs, tables and charts. However you chose to present your results, your aim must be to display your data clearly and accurately.

There are numerous types of charts and graphs, which can be used for different purposes. The types that are likely to be most useful to display information gathered during analysis of a brief or a product evaluation are:

- **Pie charts** – These compare parts to a whole and, therefore, show a percentage distribution. The entire pie represents the total data and each segment of the pie is a particular category.

The heading for your chart should always be clear.

The key for your chart should always be clear.

Do not to use too many segments in your pie chart. If there are more than six it gets far too crowded and you should consider using a bar chart instead.

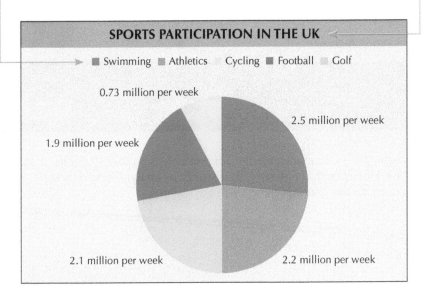

SPORTS PARTICIPATION IN THE UK

■ Swimming ■ Athletics   Cycling ■ Football ■ Golf

0.73 million per week

2.5 million per week

1.9 million per week

2.1 million per week

2.2 million per week

As with most charts and graphs, pie charts can be created in 3D.

You can emphasise segments by detaching them from each other. You may also detach a single segment to emphasise important data.

YEAR 5 BOYS' FAVOURITE COLOURS

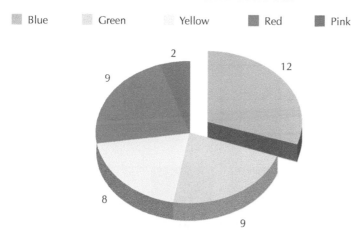

- **Line graphs** – These are most useful for showing trends in continuous data. For example, the graph shown plots the sales of iPhones over a number of years. Information like this could be used to allow the manufacturer and retailers to plan production and purchase of stock.

iPHONE SALES

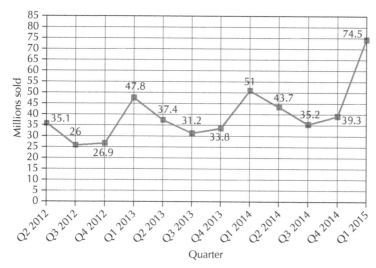

- **Bar charts** – These display data in a similar way to line graphs. However, the data is not continuous. The graph below shows the opinions of 20 respondents when asked to choose which one of six products they preferred.

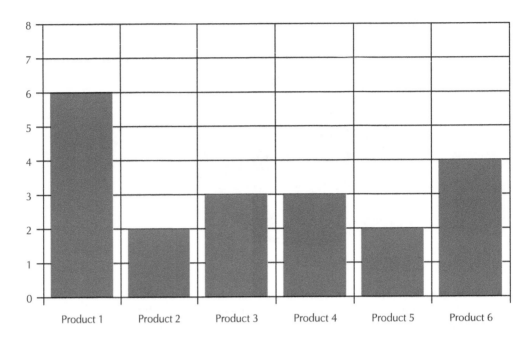

Whatever method(s) you chose to display your results, there are a few points to remember:

- Only display data graphically if this will make it clearer. For example, don't use a bar graph to compare two values that only differ by a tiny amount.
- Clearly label the graph and its axes.
- Be careful with the use of colour – don't overdo it.
- Use the same scales for related results, otherwise the data will look distorted.

Skill builder 9.2: Gathering information

Analysing existing products is one way of generating design opportunities. Gather information on a product you are not too familiar with to identify possible design opportunities. You should use a combination of the following methods of gathering information and display your results in the form of text, tables charts and graphs.

User trial

Compile a list of interview questions that can be asked after the trial has been completed.

Ask five of your classmates to use the product. Watch them and encourage them to describe any problems they are having as they are using it. Record your observations and their comments as they use the product.

Write a summary of your conclusions of the user trial.

User trip

Carry out a user trip on the product. Record (using text, photographs or video) your experience with the product. Write a summary of your conclusions about the product. This may include:

- how well the product performed
- how easy the product was to understand and use
- any difficulties you had with the product
- how it compares with other similar products you have used
- any suggestions for improving the product.

Questionnaire

Compile and use a questionnaire to gather your classmates' opinions on the product. Your questionnaire must have at least six questions and should use a range of question styles that are most appropriate for the information you are trying to gather.

Comparison to other products

Compare a product of your choice with other similar products. Gather relevant information and present it in a table similar to the one on page 224.

10. Idea generation

There are different types of thinking skills. **Creative thinking** tends to be divergent and is used in generating and developing ideas. **Analytical thinking** tends to be convergent and focuses on the narrowing down of possibilities. Designers have to be able to shift between analytical thinking and creative thinking.

Skill builder 10.1: What type of thinker are you?

Try the following activities. You can do them on your own or with others. Compare your answers.

1. Give yourself five minutes to list as many things you can do with a brick (building a wall, house or garage all count as the same thing – that's one to start you off).

Example list on page 225

2. Give yourself five minutes to list as many benefits you can think of to making cars out of jelly.

Example list on page 225

If you are an analytical thinker, you are likely to have come up with a limited number of quite sensible suggestions. If you are a creative thinker then you are likely to have come up with lots of suggestions, some of which might be a bit unusual! Both types of thinking are important in the design process.

- Creative thinking is useful at the start of the design process, when trying to generate ideas. The secret to getting an eventual successful solution is to focus on quantity over quality at the start of the design process – generate lots of ideas.
- Analytical thinking is required when working to narrow down a range of possibilities towards a solution.

Idea generation techniques

Ideas are rarely 'flashes of brilliance'. They are often the result of hard work, perhaps using idea-generation techniques.

There are nearly 200 idea generation techniques; some can be carried out by an individual and others require groups of people.

Idea generation techniques that you may find useful are:

- analogy and technology transfer
- biomimicry
- morphological analysis
- brainstorming
- SCAMPER.

Analogy and technology transfer

An analogy or metaphor can be used to apply existing knowledge in a new context. Analogy can result in technology from one product being used to solve a problem with another. This is known as technology transfer. There are lots of examples where commercial companies have used technology transfer.

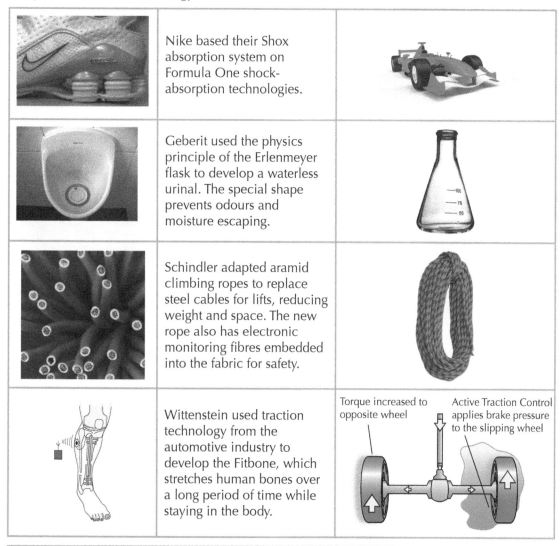

	Nike based their Shox absorption system on Formula One shock-absorption technologies.	
	Geberit used the physics principle of the Erlenmeyer flask to develop a waterless urinal. The special shape prevents odours and moisture escaping.	
	Schindler adapted aramid climbing ropes to replace steel cables for lifts, reducing weight and space. The new rope also has electronic monitoring fibres embedded into the fabric for safety.	
	Wittenstein used traction technology from the automotive industry to develop the Fitbone, which stretches human bones over a long period of time while staying in the body.	Torque increased to opposite wheel. Active Traction Control applies brake pressure to the slipping wheel

Skill builder 10.2: Technology transfer

Carry out research into how technology, materials or manufacturing methods used in one product have been applied to improve or create another product.

1. Create a poster that shows the products and how the technology transfer has been used.

OR

2. Produce a presentation about the products to show your classmates.

Example answer on page 226

Biomimicry

Ideas can be generated by using analogies with nature. This is known as biomimicry.

There are lots of examples of products that have been inspired by animals, plants and microbes.

The Japanese Shinkansen Bullet Train is the fastest train in the world, travelling at 200 miles per hour. A major problem to be solved with its design was sonic boom, which was produced when the train emerged from a tunnel as a result of air being compressed. The designers noted that kingfishers are able to dive from the air into water with very little splash compared to similar sized birds. The designers based the nose cone of the train on the beak of the kingfisher to overcome the noise problem.

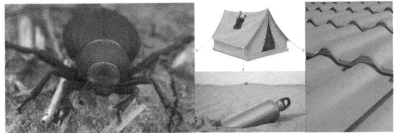

The Namib Desert beetle (above) survives in its arid habitat by harvesting moisture from the air, first by getting it to condense on its back and then by storing the water. This approach has inspired the development of a range of products, including a self-filling water bottle, and tent coverings and roof tiles that collect water.

Geckos can walk along walls and ceilings because there are millions of tiny adhesive hairs of the bottom of their toes. When the direction of the hairs is changed, the grip is instantly broken without any tearing or residue. A team of University of Massachusetts Amherst researchers developed GeckSkin™ an adhesive so strong that an index-card sized strip can hold over 300kg on a smooth surface such as glass. The ability to use a pair of gecko-inspired gloves to scale walls like Spiderman may not be far away!

Biomimicry can inspire functional and aesthetic aspects of products. An example of this is the Bird Skull Shoe by Dutch fashion designer Marieka Ratsma and American architect Kostika Spaho.

A range of techniques was used in the development of this product, including biomimicry, freehand sketches, CAD and rapid prototyping.

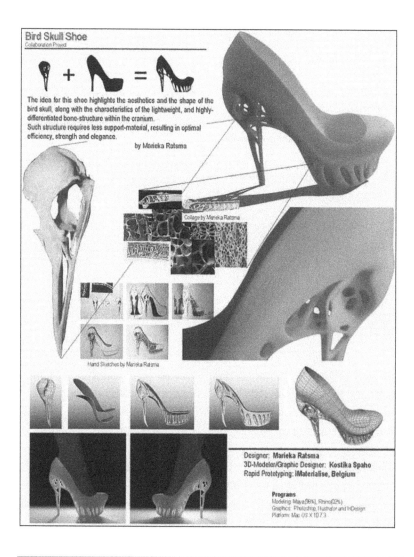

Skill builder 10.3: Biomimicry

Carry out research into how biomimicry has been used to inspire new products or new approaches. Select a product (this may already be in use or under development) that interests you and create a display poster, similar to the one for the Bird Skull Shoe, that gives details of the product and how it was inspired by biomimicry.

Example answer on page 227

Morphological analysis

Morphological analysis is a method that involves a systematic approach to the development of ideas, working with the help of a matrix. It is particularly suitable for people who are used to thinking in analytical terms.

The problem is broken down into **parameters** that are given a range of **attributes** and arranged in a matrix.

Example

To generate ideas for a new coffee table, the parameters could be number of legs, material, height and shape of top. A matrix is then created with these parameters as headings and possible attributes populating the rows (see below).

	No. of legs	Material	Height (cm)	Shape of top
1	6	Plastic	0	Triangle
2	4	Wood	10	Rectangle
3	3	Metal	30	Circle
4	2	Glass	40	Square
5	0	Wood + Metal	50	Tear Drop
6	100	Metal + Glass	60	Oval

The next stage is to generate combinations of the attributes. In this example there are 1926 ($6 \times 6 \times 6 \times 6$) possible combinations.

The combinations can be generated by selecting interesting-looking combinations or at random.

Random combinations can be generated in a number of ways, such as by asking your friend to give you a series of numbers between 1 and 6 or by using an online random number generator.

Numbers 6, 1, 4, 2 would generate a rectangular, plastic table with 100 legs at a height of 40cm.

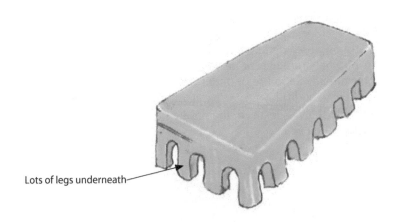

Lots of legs underneath

Random combinations of attributes can be repeated as often as required to give a range of ideas.

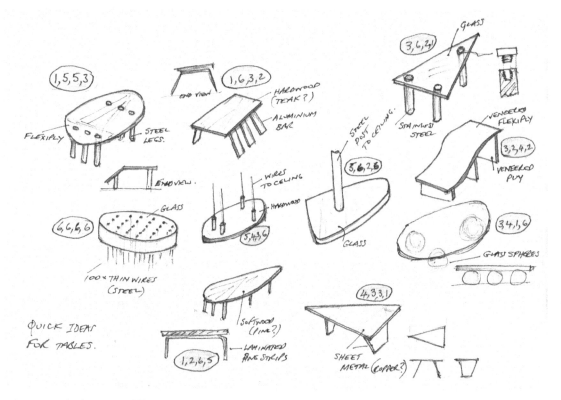

This example shows 10 different combinations randomly generated from the matrix.

Remember

- These are only initial ideas – they can be used to spark other ideas.
- Quantity is more important than quality at this stage – time should be spent generating ideas (some of which may not be practical), not perfecting graphics.
- Morphological analysis can also be used during the development of the proposal, particularly during the exploration phase.

Skill builder 10.4: Morphological analysis

Use the morphological analysis matrix below to generate a range of ideas for a toothbrush holder. Take 20 minutes for this task.

	Material	Wall/ freestanding	No. of brushes	Angle of brush
1	Metal	Wall	1	Horizontal
2	Plastic	FS	2	Vertical
3	Wood	Wall	3	Diagonal
4	Ceramic	FS	4	Mixed

Example answer on page 228

75

Brainstorming

Brainstorming, sometimes called thought showering, is an idea generation technique that encourages people to come up with ideas that can, at first, seem strange or even useless. However, these ideas can be used to spark off other ideas.

Brainstorming is often done by groups of people but can be carried out by individuals.

For brainstorming to be successful a few rules should be followed.

- Throw in as many ideas as possible.
- Don't make judgements (positive or negative) about of any of the ideas during the session.

Ideas can be evaluated, explored and refined at the end of the session.

When setting up a group brainstorming session there are several things to consider.

- How will the problem be presented? Participants need to be clear about what the problem is and that the aim of the session is to generate as many ideas as possible to solve the problem.
- How long will the session last? Although this can be flexible it is useful to set a specific time. This will depend on a number of factors, including time available, complexity of problem and number of participants.
- Who will take part? It is often better to have a diverse group as more creative ideas may be generated. Participants with different experiences, interests and skills will bring different ideas to the session.
- How will ideas be recorded? Lists, mind maps and sketches on a white board, flip charts or post-it notes are common recording methods.
- Who will record the ideas? It is difficult to record and direct the session at the same time so it is better to assign somebody to take notes.
- How will the participants be managed? Everyone, including the quietest people, must be encouraged to contribute and discouraged from criticising ideas. Creativity should be welcomed and everyone should be prompted to come up with as many ideas as possible.

Example

A group of pupils was asked to consider the following problem:

It is your best friend's birthday. They bought you an expensive present for your recent birthday. However, you have been overspending lately and only have £4.56 in your bank. How could you treat your friend for their birthday?

The pupils brainstormed the problem for 15 minutes and recorded their ideas in the form of the mindmap shown below.

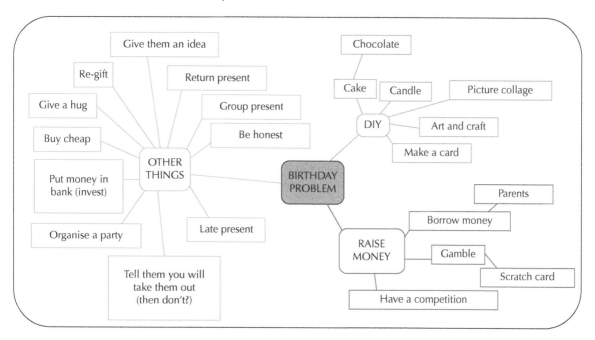

One pupil recorded all of the ideas. The next stage would be to evaluate, explore and refine the ideas put forward.

Class activity: Brainstorming picture display

A company is looking for new ways of displaying photographs (up to 10 photographs at a time). Materials available are acrylic sheets, strips of wood (50 × 10 mm), strips of aluminium (50 × 10 mm) and copper sheets.

Brainstorm possible ideas for methods of displaying the photographs.

SCAMPER

SCAMPER is an acronym for a technique that helps people think of ideas. It is particularly useful for exploring your initial ideas.

Each letter of the acronym represents a different way of approaching the exploration, as shown in the table below.

Letter	Represents	Example
S	**Substitute** one thing for another	Replace some parts, materials or processes
C	**Combine** with other functions, materials or things	Combine two very different functions in one product, combine unusual parts with other products or ideas
A	**Adapt** an existing idea	Adapt an existing product, process or idea so that it can be used for other things
M	**Modify** elements of the design	Make components larger, smaller, stronger
P	**Put** to another use	Consider other uses and other people who may use the product in a different way
E	**Eliminate** some parts of the design	Simplify, reduce or eliminate non-essential components
R	**Rearrange** sections	Reverse, rotate or move parts around

SCAMPER, like all idea generation techniques is intended to boost the creative process. It is not rigid. The letters do not need to be used in order, every letter does not have to be used and some may be used more than once.

More emphasis may be put on some letters, depending on the design task.

Example

The example below shows how SCAMPER could be used to help generate further ideas from one of the initial ideas for the toothbrush holder from Skill builder 10.4.

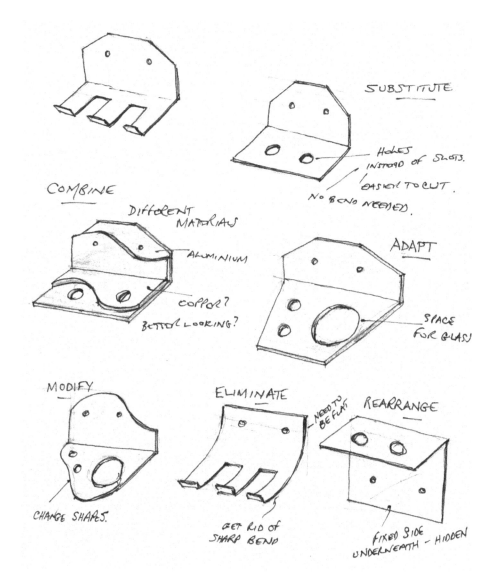

Some ideas that are generated using SCAMPER may be impractical. Don't worry about this. A crazy idea might prove to be a starting point for something innovative but more practical. The aim is to generate as many ideas as you can.

Class activity: SCAMPER

Use SCAMPER to develop one of the ideas for the toothbrush holder generated in Skill builder 10.4.

11. Development

Initial ideas are generated quickly with some regard given for the design specification. Further work is required to bring them in line with the specification and generate the level of detail required to permit manufacture. Development is the *evolution* of the design from its initial idea to final design proposal.

Development requires two key skills – **exploring** and **refining**.

Following initial idea generation, the designer considers the most promising ideas by referencing the specification. This highlights areas for improvement. **Exploration** of these areas takes place and the designer generates alternate solutions to improve them. Further use of idea generation techniques will help the designer to be creative in the exploration of solutions.

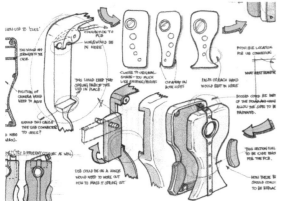

Potential solutions are investigated, tested and evaluated, with the most promising being further developed and incorporated into the design. This leads to the narrowing down and **refinement** of solutions. More specific details, such as sizes, costs, materials and suitability for manufacturing, are also likely to be tested and evaluated before being confirmed as the development progresses.

Exploring and refining should not be viewed as a linear process. It is likely that, in refining an idea, further problems or areas for improvement will arise. For example, changes to improve function will likely raise issues with aesthetics, materials and manufacturing. These new issues will require exploring, testing, evaluating and refining.

Skill builder 11.1: Planning the development of initial ideas

An initial idea for an alarm clock is shown below. Take five minutes to list as many possible areas for development that would make it more suitable for a teenage market.

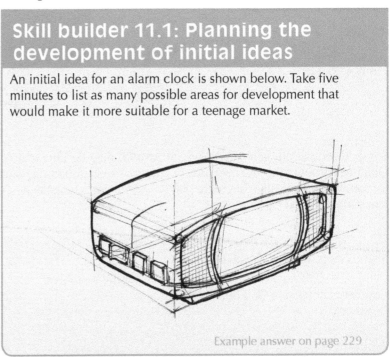

Example answer on page 229

Exploring

Exploring requires the effective application of divergent thinking (see page 70) and problem solving skills. Focus, at this point, is on generating, testing and evaluating different solutions that address any issues with the initial idea. Idea generation techniques such as SCAMPER (page 78) can help with this.

The early stages of development of a toothbrush holder are shown below. The designer has begun by exploring different ways of improving the function of the holder to make it hold toothbrushes more securely. You will see that some of the exploration has been tested using models.

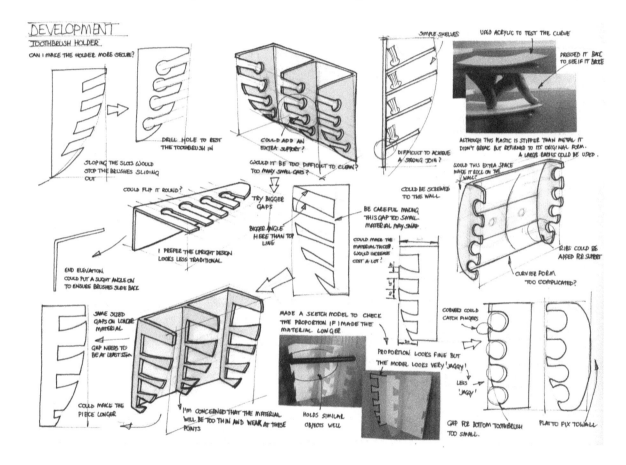

Although exploration is a creative process, solutions should be based on a sound understanding of the design issues relevant to the development and use of the product. Multiple possible solutions can be considered for each relevant issue.

Exploration should also consider suitable materials and manufacturing processes.

Exploration in action

The extracts shown (from the example on page 81) highlight some of the exploration carried out by the designer.

The designer explores improvements to the function. Different ways of holding the toothbrush have been suggested.

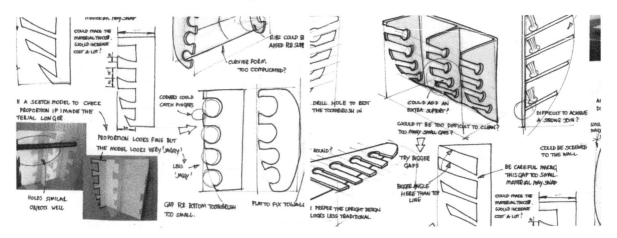

Note that some of the exploration is quite subtle and limited to simple changes in the shape. Other changes are looked at in more detail and are even modelled.

Exploring to this depth allows the designer to effectively evaluate the proposed improvement. In this instance, the change has provided greater security for the item being held.

The model highlights another issue. The designer believes that there is now a problem with the aesthetics of the toothbrush holder ('line is too jagged'). This may have come about as a result of the idea being viewed in 3D for the first time. The designer explores ways of introducing a more curvy and flowing look.

In making this change the designer has created new problems, which must be explored and resolved.

The remainder of the development is detailed on pages 84–87.

Skill builder 11.2: Exploring designs 1

Refer to the example folio displayed on pages 86 and 87.

* Identify **three** issues, other than the one already discussed, that the designer has explored.

Example answer on page 229

Skill builder 11.3: Exploring designs 2

Following the idea generation example (page 79) the designer wishes to develop the idea shown below.

- Refer to the specification below and choose **two** issues with the design that could be explored.
- Explore each of these using appropriate sketches and annotations.

No detailed refinement is required. Simply explore each issue and provide changes or more detail to the initial idea. Not all changes will lead to improvements.

Product Specification

The holder must:

1. hold four toothbrushes (maximum size of Ø10 x 220)

2. be wall mounted

3. be easy to install

4. be easy to clean

5. appeal to a high-end market

6. be made from two different materials.

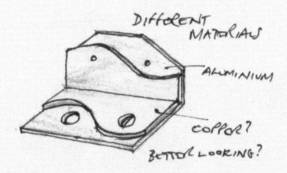

Example answer on page 229

Refining

Refining requires convergent, analytical thinking (see page 70). The focus is on making decisions and providing enough detail to permit the manufacture of the product. The range of solutions and information generated from exploring is narrowed down or synthesised, tested and evaluated.

Effective refinement leads to a design that meets the specification. Materials and manufacturing processes will be suitable and justified.

Being able to *apply* knowledge and understanding of design issues and materials and manufacturing processes is key to effective refinement.

The latter stages of development for the toothbrush holder from page 81 are shown below.

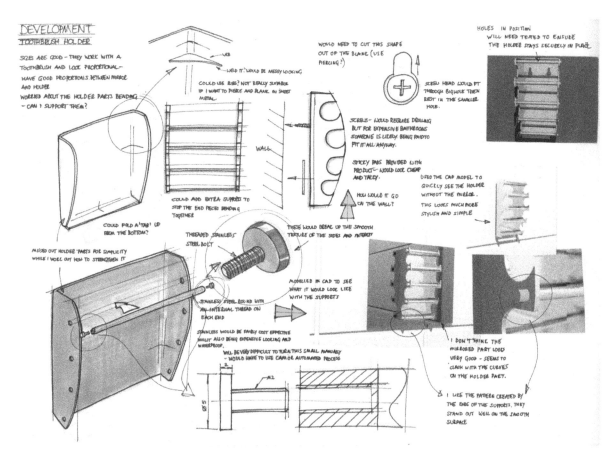

Firstly, it should be noted that exploration is still taking place. Even at this advanced stage the designer is still discovering issues that require further investigation. However, in refining the idea the designer is recording more intricate details of the design such as the key sizes of components, material choices and the manufacturing processes that will be used to create them.

Refining in action

The extracts shown (from the example on page 84) highlight some of the refinement carried out by the designer.

Important sizes have been recorded. A sectional sketch has been used to communicate and record dimensions and the assembly method of one of the component parts. The annotations surrounding the sketch suggest the materials that the designer is considering.

An exploded sketch has been used to detail how the component parts will be assembled. This level of detail was not required from previous graphics during the idea generation and exploration activities. An enlarged view indicates that one component will have a thread cut on it. Again, annotations are used to provide further detail such as materials and processes.

A scale model has been made using the refined sizes. The designer can therefore also evaluate the proportion. The production of the model also allows the designer to test the assembly.

Other details still require refining. These might include materials and manufacturing costs and production planning.

The remainder of the development is detailed on pages 86 and 87.

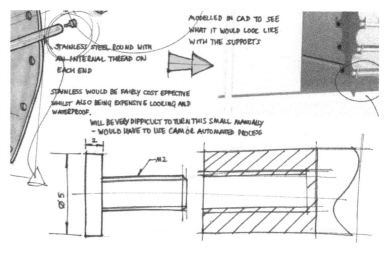

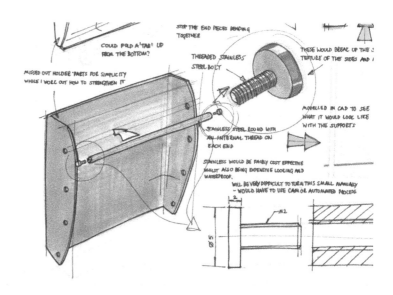

Skill builder 11.4: Refining designs

Refer to the example folio displayed on pages 86 and 87.

- Identify **three** aspects, other than the one already discussed, that the designer has refined.
- Carry out refinement for the toothbrush idea you explored in Skill builder 11.3 (page 83).

Example answer on page 229

Complete development of toothbrush holder

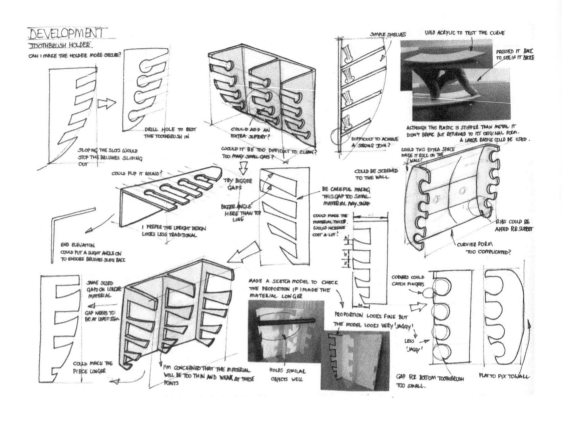

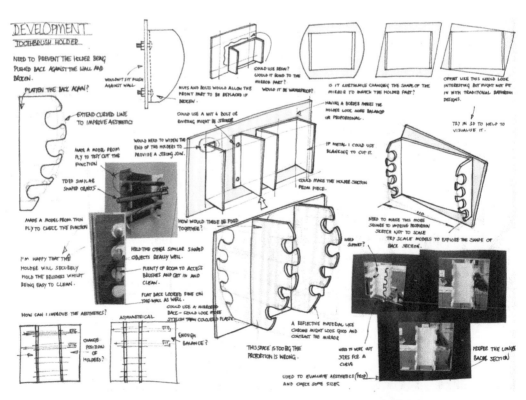

DEVELOPMENT
TOOTHBRUSH HOLDER

SIZES ARE GOOD - THEY WORK WITH A TOOTHBRUSH AND LOOK PROPORTIONAL - HAVE GOOD PROPORTIONS BETWEEN MIRROR AND HOLDER

WORRIED ABOUT THE HOLDER PARTS BENDING - CAN I SUPPORT THEM?

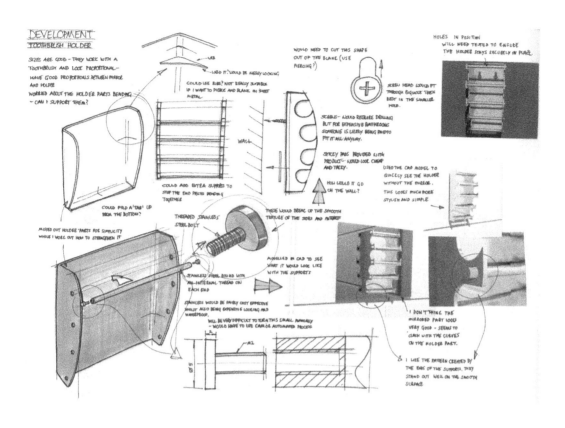

COULD FOLD A 'TAB' UP FROM THE BOTTOM?

MISSED OUT HOLDER 'PARTS FOR SIMPLICITY WHILE I WORK OUT HOW TO STRENGTHEN IT

THREADED STAINLESS STEEL BOLT

STAINLESS STEEL ROUND WITH AN INTERNAL THREAD ON EACH END

STAINLESS WOULD BE FAIRLY COST EFFECTIVE WHILST ALSO BEING EXPENSIVE LOOKING AND WATERPROOF. WILL BE VERY DIFFICULT TO TURN THIS SMALL ANOMALY - WOULD HAVE TO USE CAM OR AUTOMATED PROCESS

COULD USE RIBS? NOT REALLY SUITABLE UP I WANT TO PIERCE AND BLANK IN SHEET METAL

RIB

USED IT. WOULD BE MESSY LOOKING

COULD ADD EXTRA SUPPORT TO STOP THE END PIECES BENDING TOGETHER

WALL

WOULD NEED TO CUT THIS SHAPE OUT OF THE BLANK (USE PIERCING?)

SCREW HEAD WOULD FIT THROUGH BIG HOLE THEN REST IN THE SMALLER HOLE.

SCREWS - WOULD REQUIRE DRILLING BUT FOR EXPENSIVE BATHROOMS SOMEONE IS LIKELY BEING PAID TO FIT IT ALL ANYWAY.

STICKY PADS PROVIDED WITH PRODUCT - WOULD LOOK CHEAP AND TACKY.

HOW WOULD IT GO ON THE WALL?

THESE WOULD BREAK UP THE SMOOTH TEXTURE OF THE SIDES AND INTEREST

MODELLED IN CAD TO SEE WHAT IT WOULD LOOK LIKE WITH THE SUPPORTS

HOLES IN POSITION WILL NEED TESTED TO ENSURE THE HOLDER STAYS SECURELY IN PLACE.

USED THE CAD MODEL TO QUICKLY SEE THE HOLDER WITHOUT THE MIRROR. THIS LOOKS MUCH MORE STYLISH AND SIMPLE

I DON'T THINK THE MIRRORED PART LOOKS VERY GOOD - SEEMS TO CLASH WITH THE CURVES ON THE HOLDER PART.

I LIKE THE PATTERN CREATED BY THE ENDS OF THE SUPPORTS. THEY STAND OUT WELL ON THE SMOOTH SURFACE

DEVELOPMENT
TOOTHBRUSH HOLDER

I WILL USE THE SIZES FROM MY MODELS TO PRODUCE A SCALE DRAWING OF THE BLANK.

※ STAINLESS STEEL WILL BE USED - THIS HAS AN EXCELLENT & VERY ATTRACTIVE FINISH, COLOUR AND REFLECTION. IT WILL PROVIDE VERY GOOD RESISTANCE TO CORROSION. IT CAN BE CUT USING BLANKING THEN FORCED OR PRESS FORMED.

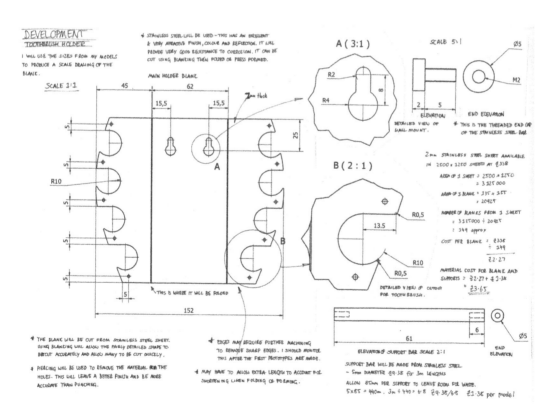

MAIN HOLDER BLANK

SCALE 1:1

A (3:1)
DETAILED VIEW OF WALL MOUNT.

SCALE 5:1
ELEVATION
END ELEVATION
※ THIS IS THE THREADED END CAP OF THE STAINLESS STEEL BAR.

B (2:1)
DETAILED VIEW OF CUTOUT FOR TOOTHBRUSH.

2mm STAINLESS STEEL SHEET AVAILABLE IN 2500 x 1250 SHEETS AT £338.

AREA OF 1 SHEET = 2500 x 1250
= 3 125 000

AREA OF 1 BLANK = 135 x 155
= 20925

NUMBER OF BLANKS FROM 1 SHEET
= 3125000 ÷ 20925
= 149 approx

COST PER BLANK = £338
÷ 149
£2·27

MATERIAL COST FOR BLANK AND SUPPORTS = £2·27 + £1·38
= £3·65

ELEVATION OF SUPPORT BAR SCALE 2:1
END ELEVATION

SUPPORT BAR WILL BE MADE FROM STAINLESS STEEL
- 5mm DIAMETER £9·38 for 3m LENGTHS
ALLOW 85mm PER SUPPORT TO LEAVE ROOM FOR WASTE.
5 x 85 = 440m. 3m ÷ 440 = 6·8 £9·38/6·8 = £1·38 per model!

※ THE BLANK WILL BE CUT FROM STAINLESS STEEL SHEET. USING BLANKING WILL ALLOW THE FAIRLY DETAILED SHAPE TO BE CUT ACCURATELY AND ALLOW MANY TO BE CUT QUICKLY.

※ PIERCING WILL BE USED TO REMOVE THE MATERIAL FOR THE HOLES. THIS WILL LEAVE A BETTER FINISH AND BE MORE ACCURATE THAN PUNCHING.

※ EDGES MAY REQUIRE FURTHER MACHINING TO REMOVE SHARP EDGES. I SHOULD MONITOR THIS AFTER THE FIRST PROTOTYPES ARE MADE.

※ MAY HAVE TO ALLOW EXTRA LENGTH TO ACCOUNT FOR SHORTENING WHEN FOLDING OR FORMING.

12. Written communication

In design tasks, written communication normally takes the form of annotations. Annotations are short notes and comments that are used to explain specific aspects of the design. They should usually be attached to specific graphics (including images of models) but can also be used in isolation as a quick method of recording details or changes.

Annotations can be used for a variety of purposes. They should always communicate detail that is not immediately obvious from looking at the graphic or model. Otherwise the designer is simply duplicating information that is already available.

Skill builder 12.1: Identifying effective annotating

An initial idea for a desktop speaker is shown with annotations.

- Identify **three** annotations that are useful and justify your choices.
- Select **three** that are not useful and explain your choice.

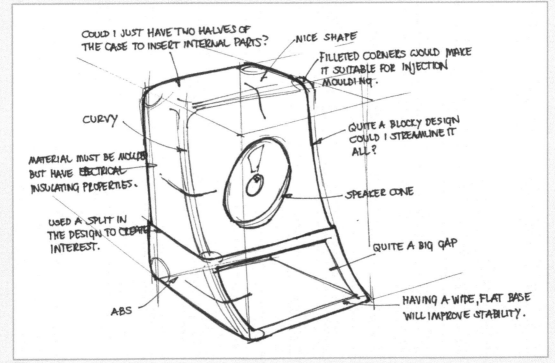

Example answers on page 230

Written communication is used for a number of reasons.

Referencing the design specification

Throughout the design process, annotations can be used to communicate the links between ideas and the specification.

Graphics and models that are used to communicate initial ideas can lack detail and be rough or simplistic. Further detail can be added, with little extra time needed, through annotations. Notes and comments can quickly clarify the designer's thinking as to how that idea fulfils the brief or specification.

Referencing design, materials and manufacturing issues

The designer regularly **evaluates** ideas in terms of design factors and the suitability of certain materials and manufacturing processes. Again, notes and comments can quickly be used to communicate the designer's thoughts.

It is important to think of annotations as the *application* of your knowledge and understanding to inform your decision making. They are not statements to be forgotten!

Recording decisions

As a design evolves, the designer will use annotations to record their decision-making process.

For example, during exploration activity, annotations may be in the form of **questions** or **prompts**. The designer may question certain design decisions, highlighting areas for improvement or further exploration.

In reply to these questions, and during refinement activity, the designer may record their answers and related decisions. Annotations like this will help to communicate the designer's thought process and show that decisions have been reached through effective exploration and refinement.

Using annotations effectively in the Higher Design and Manufacture course is an excellent way of demonstrating knowledge and understanding of design factors and materials and manufacturing.

Skill builder 12.2: Using written communication

Create a sketch of an everyday product.

Annotate it to communicate additional information such as design factors and materials and manufacturing processes.

Example answers on page 230

13. Application of graphics

The role of graphics in the design process

Graphics, and in particular drawings and sketches, are the quickest method of communicating design work.

Designers employ a wide variety of drawings and sketches to communicate their ideas. Some of these are shown in the table below.

Graphic Type	Purpose
Rough 2D/3D sketch	Quickly record generated ideas or develop ideas.
Orthographic sketch	To provide detail such as dimensions.
Oblique sketch/drawing	Three-dimensional graphics used to better visualise an idea or when sharing with non-experts.
One-point perspective sketch/drawing	
Isometric sketch/ drawing	
Two-point perspective sketch/drawing	
Exploded/assembled sketches/drawing	To show how different components fit together (in 2D or 3D).
Sectional sketch/drawing	To communicate the interior of ideas (cutaways can also be shown in 3D).
Scale drawing	To better visualise size and proportion. To work out sizes and ensure fit for assembly.
Working drawing	Provided to the manufacturer to facilitate manufacture.
Manual rendered illustration	To communicate the final design proposal to the client.
CAD drawing	

The graphic type used, and its visual quality, will depend upon the stage of the design process being undertaken. The graphic type used should always be appropriate for the task.

For example, during the generation of ideas the designer will use quick, rough sketches to record their thoughts. These will be clear enough for the designer to understand but it is not necessary for a client or non-expert to understand them. A detailed rendered image would be more appropriate and better visualised by the client and is normally used when presenting a design proposal.

Freehand sketching

Freehand sketching is a method of recording and communicating your thoughts quickly on paper.

Freehand sketching is normally performed unaided by drawing equipment such as rulers and compasses, which only serve to slow the process down. As a result, the appearance of freehand sketches lacks the accuracy of drawings completed with drawing equipment or CAD. Nevertheless, sketches must still be clear and suitable for their intended purpose.

Basic sketching technique

Developing an effective sketching technique will greatly help you in the Design and Manufacture course. Take some time to think about how you sketch.

All sketches are made up of lines and arcs and the ability to sketch these is therefore very important. There are many exercises available that will help develop these skills and they can be found using a quick internet search or by asking your teacher.

In summary, the following should be considered and practised:

- Sit in an upright position that allows the whole sketching area to be viewed.
- Be aware of how you use your arm. Movement in the wrist and elbow will cause lines to be curvy. Limiting movement in the wrist and elbow will help when sketching straight lines. Movement should mainly come **from the shoulder**.
- Perform a practice movement of the line or arc prior to actually sketching it. This is called **ghosting**.
- Lines should be sketched long, smoothly and with confidence. Longer lines should not be made up of lots of shorter *hairy* lines.
- Try to sketch lines with the same action. Normally (for right-handed people) this is a left-to-right action sketched at an angle of roughly 45° to your body. Turn the page to sketch lines in a different direction – do not change your action.

Some examples of sketching exercises. Top: practising straight lines and moving the paper. Bottom: sketching and combining simple shapes.

Class activity: Basic sketching technique

On a piece of blank paper practise sketching lines, arcs and circles using the technique above. Replicate the exercises shown in the examples. Focus on your sketching action. Persevere if it feels awkward. Evaluate yourself against the criteria listed above.

Two dimensional graphics

Sketching in only two dimensions provides the quickest and easiest method of recording ideas on paper. The quick pace at which it can be carried out makes it ideal for idea generation or when developing a visually complex idea that you can't fully visualise or sketch yet in 3D.

An important aspect of sketching in two dimensions begins with the ability to analyse a product and break it down into its component shapes.

Analysis of the above toy robot, for example, would provide a series of lines, squares, rectangles, circles and triangles.

These shapes would initially be sketched using light lines – **construction lines**. The designer would make regular checks and corrections to the proportion to ensure the design is visually correct.

The designer would then combine the shapes and tidy up the sketch by drawing heavier outlines. Lines that only serve as construction (lines used to line shapes up, leftovers from combinations or overlaps) are ignored during outlining.

Sketching these shapes alone would provide a fairly simplistic, child-like sketch. It is important to add detail. In this instance details such as buttons, rivets, dials and gauges would be added. Corners would also be rounded slightly.

Skill builder 13.1: Sketching in 2D

Analyse the toy robot shown above. Identify and practise sketching the shapes that it is made from.

Sketch a range of robots similar to the one shown. Make sure to use the basic sketching technique described and to begin each sketch using construction lines and shapes. Consider using an idea generation technique. See pages 70–79.

Example answers on page 231

Three dimensional graphic styles

The human eye views the world in three dimensions, which makes 3D graphics types easier and quicker to understand. There are different methods that can be used to create 3D graphics.

Oblique sketching and drawing

Oblique is the most simple 3D graphic type to produce. The elevation of a component or product is drawn or sketched then the sides are projected back at an angle (normally 45°). To preserve proportions a half scale is normally adopted on any part of the sketch being projected back.

Oblique projection can be used to quickly transform a 2D shape into a 3D form and is therefore best suited for initial design tasks such as idea generation and exploration. Circles can be difficult to sketch on projected faces.

When choosing a graphic technique for a more detailed or realistic sketch then isometric or perspective graphic types provide better options.

An oblique view sketched during idea generation for a storage rack for console games.

Isometric sketching and drawing

Isometric is a versatile graphic type that is commonly used throughout the design process.

It differs from oblique in that an angle (30°) is applied to both sides. Also, the length, depth and height of the product are all sketched with the same scale (hence the *iso* part of the name).

Isometric views are traditionally created using the drawing board and drawing equipment. They can be tricky to sketch freehand. To make it easier a technique called *crating* is used.

Crating is done using the following steps:

- Using construction lines an isometric cube is sketched with the same major dimensions or proportion as the product.
- The elevation of the product is sketched onto the appropriate face of the crate.
- Corners are projected back and detail is outlined on the other two faces.
- Lines used for *edges* (as opposed to *corners*) are made heavier to give depth.

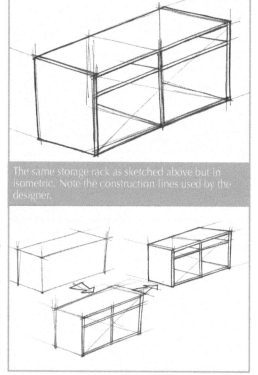

The same storage rack as sketched above but in isometric. Note the construction lines used by the designer.

Perspective

One- and two-point perspective views take into account the important fact that as objects move further away from us they become smaller. This is known as foreshortening. Also, depending upon the angle we view the object from, some distances can become distorted.

Sketches created in perspective are more pleasing to the human eye and therefore are more commonly used than other 3D graphic types by designers. Perspective, and in particular two-point perspective, is the most realistic view you can use to communicate your ideas.

Crating is useful when sketching in perspective.

Again, many one- and two-point sketching exercises can be found by searching online or by asking your teacher.

Directions on how to sketch a two-point perspective crate are provided below.

Start by sketching a vertical line to represent the leading edge of the crate (the corner nearest you). Mark how tall you want the cube to be along this line.

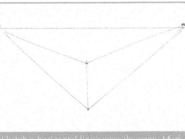

Sketch a horizontal line across the page. Mark points on this line near both sides of the page (vanishing points). Join these with the height points on the leading edge.

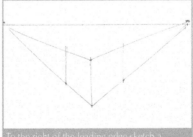

To the right of the leading edge sketch a vertical line indicating how wide the crate should be and to the left sketch another vertical for the width.

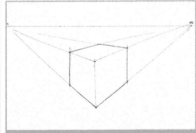

Where the vertical to the right touches the height line sketch a line towards the left-hand vanishing point. Repeat for the left-hand vertical and right-hand vanishing point.

Skill builder 13.2: Crating

On a blank piece of paper practise crating. Sketch a series of two-point perspective cubes in various positions all relative to the same eye level and vanishing points.

Example answers on page 231

Most products do not completely resemble simple cubes however. The same process of analysis used in visualising products in 2D should be applied when sketching in perspective or other 3D styles.

Break the product being sketched into simple forms or break down the initial sketched crate using construction lines.

It can sometimes be helpful to treat individual faces of a 3D form as a 2D sketch and project this sketch to a vanishing point to achieve perspective.

The guide below demonstrates how these techniques can be applied to sketch an everyday product like the digital alarm clock pictured to the right.

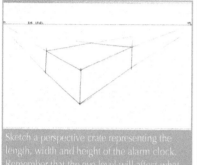

Sketch a perspective crate representing the length, width and height of the alarm clock. Remember that the eye level will affect what is seen.

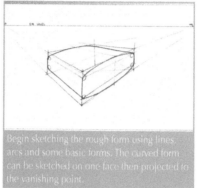

Begin sketching the rough form using lines, arcs and some basic forms. The curved form can be sketched on one face then projected to the vanishing point.

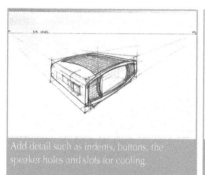

Add detail such as indents, buttons, the speaker holes and slots for cooling.

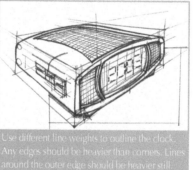

Use different line weights to outline the clock. Any edges should be heavier than corners. Lines around the outer edge should be heavier still.

Skill builder 13.3: Simple products in perspective

Sketch a range of interesting forms, in perspective, that could be used as the main body of a digital alarm clock. Add some detail such as buttons, displays, speakers, joins, fixings and feet.

This should be done at pace. Try to fill a side of paper with several sketches.

Example answers on page 232

Applying your graphic skills

You will be assessed on your ability to *select* and *use* appropriate graphic techniques to represent your ideas and proposals in 2D and 3D.

Remember though, the assessment is not about your ability to create visually impressive graphics. You will be assessed on whether your application of graphic techniques is relevant and suitable for the task being undertaken.

Of course, in order to produce the necessary range of graphic types you will have to develop your skills in this area.

Using appropriate graphic techniques

The examples below, for a toothbrush holder, demonstrate how graphics might differ throughout the design folio.

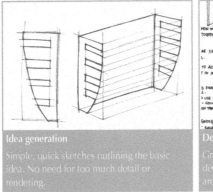

Idea generation
Simple, quick sketches outlining the basic idea. No need for too much detail or rendering.

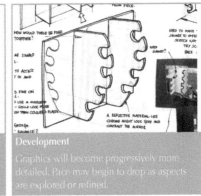

Development
Graphics will become progressively more detailed. Pace may begin to drop as aspects are explored or refined.

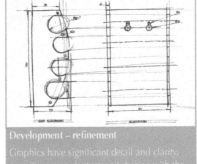

Development – refinement
Graphics have significant detail and clarity, permitting manufacture and sharing with the design team.

Presentation
Time is taken to prepare a photorealistic graphic. These are visually impressive and clear to the non-expert client.

Selecting appropriate graphic techniques

The following pages highlight the types of graphics that might be suitable for the different stages of the design process.

The focus here should be on selecting graphics that *effectively communicate* your ideas and are most suitable to the task being undertaken.

Graphics during initial idea generation

Graphics used at this stage are mainly **exploratory**. They are for personal use and, as such, presentation quality is often sacrificed for quantity of ideas and a fast pace.

Sketching will be freehand and carried out at a fast pace. Remember, the focus at this stage is upon the generation of ideas. Graphics used will have minimal detail and likely focus upon shape and form.

Graphic types will include a range of 2D and 3D styles dependent upon the complexity of the shapes and forms being sketched.

The initial ideas example shown below was produced after morphological analysis (shown to the right). The designer chose to refine some of the ideas for clarity and to add detail.

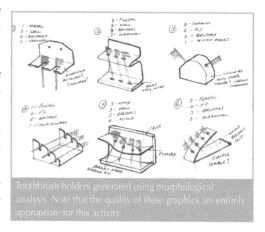

Toothbrush holders generated using morphological analysis. Note that the quality of these graphics are entirely appropriate for this activity.

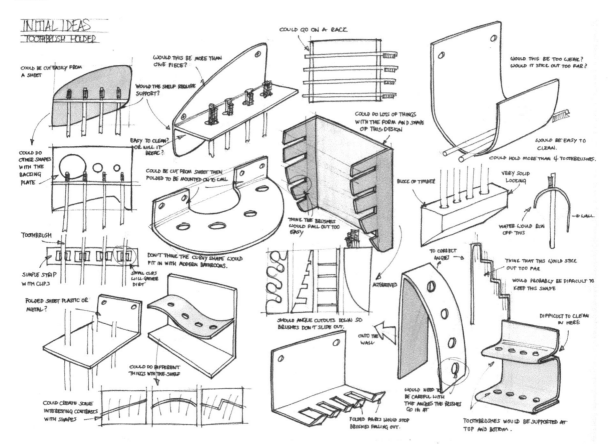

The example above has been produced at a fast pace. The designer was very skilled and capable of producing graphics of this quality quickly. Your graphics do not have to be of this visual quality at this stage. You are free to do so however, should you have the skill.

Graphics during development

An explanation of the development stage/process can be found on pages 80–87.

The graphic types, and quality, used should be suitable for the two main activities being carried out – **exploring** and **refining**.

An example of the graphics used during development can be seen below and on the opposite page.

Exploring

Graphics used at this stage should be mainly exploratory. Much of the focus during this activity is on creative thinking and the time and effort spent creating graphics should not hinder this.

Sketches will continue to be used for idea generation purposes as the designer explores various solutions. As such, graphics are initially likely to be simplistic, lack detail and be completed quickly. However, the graphics used will increase in detail as the designer focuses upon certain aspects of the design.

Some explanatory graphics, such as dimensioned and exploded sketches, will be used to visualise and record emerging details.

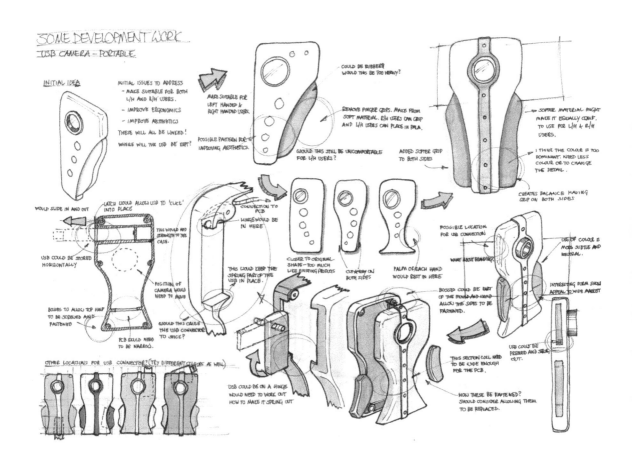

Refining

As key decisions are made then the types of graphics selected should become suitable for communicating detail. The processes leading to these decisions will be clearly recorded and communicated.

Graphics used at this stage will be mainly **explanatory**.

These might include:

- **Exploded sketches and drawings** (2D or 3D) to allow assembly methods or individual component parts to be communicated.
- **Sectional sketches and drawings** to provide information on the internal sections of the product not otherwise viewable.
- **Dimensioned orthographic sketches/drawings** providing dimensions that are to be tested or recorded final sizes.
- **Rendered views** might be created to communicate materials or aspects of the aesthetics.
- Other types of explanatory graphics such as **silhouettes** and **arrows** that provide a visual of how the product will function (if there are moving parts).

At this stage the designer is still problem solving. As a result, graphics, whilst more detailed, will still be quickly produced.

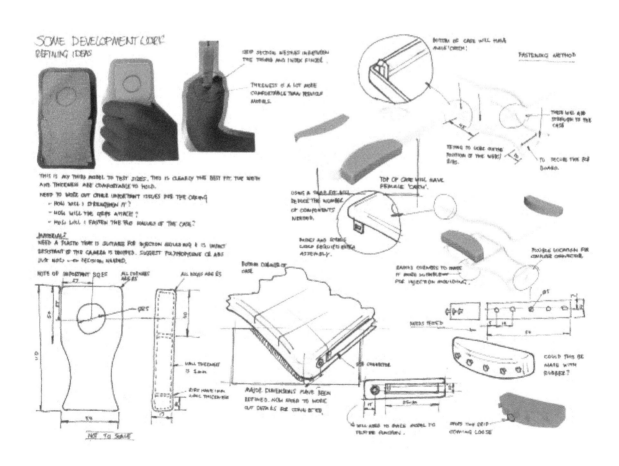

Graphics during planning for manufacture

Production graphics will mainly be used during this stage.

They will be rich in information, containing sufficient detail to allow prototypes and manufacture to take place. As such, the best format is 2D and orthographic. This type of graphic allows for a lot of detail to be presented in a clear fashion.

As these graphics will be shared with manufacturers and other members of the design team they should be accurate. They are likely to be produced with drawing equipment or using CAD software, normally to a scale. Time is taken at this stage to ensure all necessary details are recorded and communicated.

Graphic types may include:

- **Orthographic drawings** of individual components or the fully assembled product.
- **Sectioned orthographic** drawings to communicate internal details.
- **Exploded** drawings will help communicate assembly methods.

The example below shows some planning for a toothbrush holder.

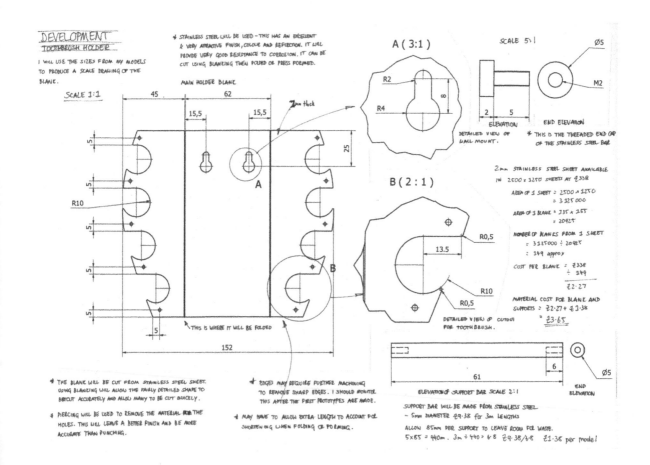

Class activity: Planning for manufacture

For the products shown below (or similar products you have in your possession), produce a variety of graphics that provide the necessary details for their manufacture.

Record dimensions, costs and assembly methods that you think might be suitable.

Graphics for communicating with a client

Graphics used at this stage are mainly **presentation** or **promotional**.

These graphics are used to communicate the design proposal to the client. A mixture of graphics types can be used, 2D or 3D. It is important to remember that the client might not be an expert and may not understand complicated technical drawings.

The use of graphics should provide the client with a clear image of what the proposal will look like and what it can do. As these graphics are used to promote your proposal to the client, or the design team, they should be visually appealing. Rendering techniques should be used to make the graphics look photorealistic.

Remember, it is likely that any presentation to the client will include the use of graphics and any prototype or presentation models.

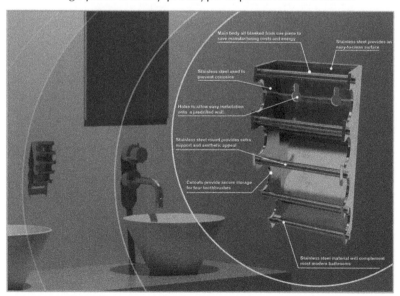

A CAD-produced presentation graphic is shown above. Accompanying notes explain how the proposal fulfils the design specification.

Rendering

Developing manual rendering skills will help you to produce graphics that are clear and communicate textures and materials. These skills can then be used quickly throughout the folio to add clarity where appropriate.

Many CAD packages now have excellent rendering facilities within them. These can be used to quickly produce professional, photorealistic graphics.

Skill builder 13.4: Light and dark rendering solutions

Sketch the forms shown below onto a piece of paper.

Using media of your choice, render each of the forms to communicate the effect of a single light source upon them.

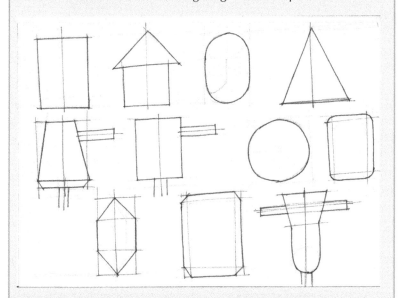

By combining forms you can build more complicated solutions that can be applied more readily to everyday products.

Example answers on page 232

14. Application of modelling

The role of modelling in the design process

Modelling plays an important part in the design process. Modelling can be used right at the beginning of the design process and continue to be applied through to planning for production.

The table below details a range of common uses of modelling. It should be noted that these are not prescriptive and a single model may be used for more than one purpose.

Uses of models	Details
Generating and exploring ideas	Modelling, like sketching, is fundamental to the generation and exploration of ideas. Models for generating and exploring ideas should be able to be produced quickly and do not require a high level of detail. Models are often used to supplement sketches but may also allow generation of ideas that are not easily sketched.
Refining	Modelling is particularly useful when refining ideas. It is often used for testing ergonomics with users. It can also be used to check any moving parts, fit of parts and manufacturing details. A large number of models are often produced during refinement, with each model building on information gained from the previous model. The starting point may be very simple models, which become more detailed and accurate as refinement takes place.
Communicating	Models are often used to communicate the final appearance and/or function of the product. They can be used to present to clients for approval before production starts. They can also be used for carrying out market research and marketing the new product. Models produced for this purpose should have high visual refinement, including precise detail such as radii, split lines and finish, including texture.
Verifying design	Modelling can be used to test many aspects of a product prior to mass production. Aspects that may be tested include aesthetics, function, fit and strength. The type of model used will depend on the aspect being tested but it should be noted that a combination of physical and digital models is often used.

Types of models

A wide range of modelling types is available to designers, including physical and digital modelling. There is also a wide range of materials that can be used to produce the models. Consideration must be given to the purpose of the model before modelling begins.

Sketch models

Sketch models are simple physical models made of low cost, easy-to-work materials. As with all models, sketch models must be made for a purpose. Sketch models can be used for a number of reasons, such as to:

- express an idea. Sketch models, like 2D sketching, can be produced very quickly to help the designer and others visualise ideas. Sketch models have the advantage that they can be handled and 'played with'.
- check product scale. Sizes and proportions can very quickly be checked with sketch models and this may help identify other issues, such as poor stability.
- explore user interaction with the idea. Sketch models can be produced to allow potential users to provide feedback.
- assess operational issues. Sketch models can be used to check early ideas for features such as levers, linkages, fitting of parts.

Any material that can be easily worked is generally suited to sketch modelling. Typical materials are card, styrofoam, foam board, modelling clay as well as some forms of wood (particularly balsa), plastics and metals. Construction kits such as Meccano® or Lego® may be useful for certain types of design tasks.

The images below show extracts from two different seating design tasks. In each, sketch models were made from readily available materials (card, acrylic and mild steel sheet) and used to explore the concepts in 3D.

Through the use of the sketch models, the designer was able to identify stability, ergonomics, performance and aesthetic issues that need to be developed further. Sketching on the photographs allowed the designer to record issues and potential changes quickly.

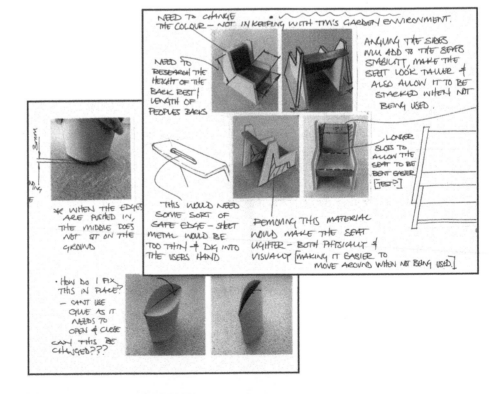

Block models

Block models are commonly used to communicate and develop the form, dimensions and surface details of the product. Block models have no internal details such as working or moving parts. They can be used to test ergonomics or present to a client for advertising. The quality of finish of the block model will depend on the purpose it is being used for. A model used to check ergonomics may be rough and unfinished whereas a model used for presentation purposes should show surface detail such as screws, split lines, texture and colour.

Block models are typically manufactured from styrofoam blocks. MDF, wood, clay or plastic sheet can also be used.

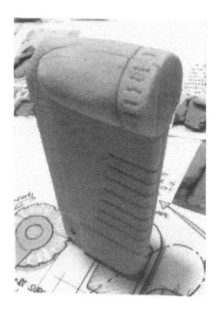

The block model of a torch, shown left, was made to test the position of the buttons and the overall feel of the product when held. This could not be done by any other method and it allowed the designer to make decisions about these features.

Another block model of the torch, shown below, was made to present to the client. Details such as split lines, colour and texture have now been added.

Working models

Working models incorporate the working or moving parts of the product.

The parts will depend on the type of model but may include levers and linkages or parts that are hinged or fitted together.

When designing an item such as a bottle opener, working models are useful to check the parts will move without interfering with each other. 2D or 3D models can be used and may be physical or computer generated.

Working models could have been used when developing this camera to check things such as the operation of the switches and the opening and closing of the shutter.

Working models of circuits of products may be constructed to not only check that they operate properly but also that they fit into place.

3D computer models

In recent years, 3D computer-generated models have become commonplace within the design industry due to their ability to be fully integrated within the CAD/CAM workplace, reducing the tooling development cost and speeding up the development stage.

The models themselves are generated using a number of different techniques, depending on the intended use of the model or the actual form of the product.

All 3D computer-modelling techniques produce digital models that only exist within the modelling application and computer hardware. These models can't be handled, but they do have a number of other valuable functions.

- Rendering applications can be used to apply surface finishes to these models, resulting in realistic images that can be used by marketing teams to communicate and evaluate in the same way that conventional manual rendering was once used. Computer modelling allows changes to the rendering to be made very quickly, enabling a large variety of combinations of colours and textures to be considered.

- Computer models allow the product to be rotated and viewed from any number of different angles with ease.

- Computer models can also be used to generate orthographic and sectional drawings to be used in the manufacture and assembly of products. As these drawings are generated directly from the 3D model, any changes made to the models are instantly updated on the working drawings.

- After the models have had specific materials' properties applied, they can then be loaded into virtual environments and simulators to evaluate how the products behave in a variety of different conditions. This feature has become well used in the construction, automotive and avionics industries to test moving parts in collision scenarios and for testing mould design.

Most schools have 3D modelling software that can be used in the Design and Manufacture course. 3D models are most likely to be used in the production of design proposals and to produce detailed working drawings.

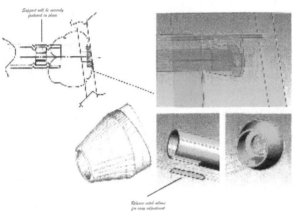

Using 3D models as part of the development helps the designer to test, develop and communicate technical details.

The images to the left show how the designer has used screenshots of the 3D model, sketching on top of them to communicate the development of the assembly and the aesthetic of the chair.

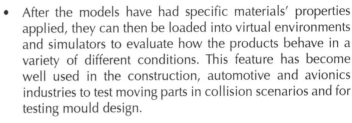

Combining manual graphics and computer models in this way allows the designer to communicate details that are not already evident in a sketch or other model. CAD modelling can be time consuming, so it is vital that these models are used to good effect. Bear in mind that there may be quicker and more effective ways of communicating some features.

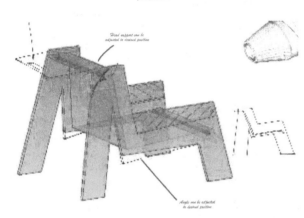

When deciding whether to use 3D CAD models you need to consider your own CAD modelling skills, time constraints and the level of detail required.

Skill builder 14.1: Computer generated modelling

The use of 3D computer models throughout the design process brings many benefits to both the manufacturer and the consumer.

Describe the benefits of using 3D computer models over traditional solid models for:

- manufacturers
- consumers.

Example answers on page 233

Rapid prototype models

Rapid prototyping is a method of making a model directly from CAD data.

Most modelling techniques are **subtractive**, the models are formed from large sheets or blocks and material is removed to leave the final form of the model. Rapid prototype modelling is referred to as an **additive** process because materials are added to the model layer by layer until the model is complete. As a result, rapid prototyping is a very efficient method of manufacturing models.

Rapid prototyping has a number of advantages such as:

- end products can be printed
- no restrictions because of mould design
- moving parts can be printed.

There is a range of rapid prototype techniques and they can be described by four major aspects:

- Input: There are two main methods to transfer the design information – using a CAD model or using a physical model. Physical models need to be converted to a digital format using a 3D scanner.
- Method: There are three main methods of rapid prototyping:
  - photo-curing – laser beam(s) or a lamp are used to cure (harden) the material
  - cutting and gluing
  - melting, solidifying and joining.
- Materials: These can come in powder, liquid or solid form. A wide range of materials are used, including plastics, wax, resins, paper and ceramics.
- Application: There is a wide range of uses for rapid prototype models and these can be grouped into design, engineering and manufacturing.

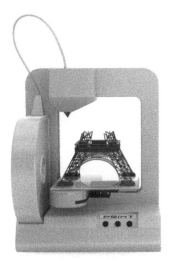 

The characteristics of a range of rapid prototyping techniques is given in the following table.

Technique	Method	Materials	Characteristics
Three-dimensional printing (3DP)	An inkjet-type printer head lays binders down on top of powdered resin to progressively build the finished shape.	Starch, ceramic, acrylic, or metal powders.	Poor surface finish. Can produce parts 250 × 200 × 200mm. Machines are relatively inexpensive. Models can be weak depending on material used.
Stereolithography (SLA)	A single laser scans across areas to harden, layer by layer.	Polymer – dependent on intended use of model, e.g. flexible, temperature resistant.	Can produce highly complex and accurate parts (+/- 0.05mm). Can produce parts 1000 × 800 × 500mm. Machines are expensive.
Selective laser sintering (SLS)	A laser traces the shape of the product layer by layer, fusing the material together to form the model.	Thermoplastic, metal or ceramic powders.	Limited accuracy (+/- 0.1mm). Can produce parts 700 × 500 × 450mm. Machines are expensive.
Fused deposition modelling (FDM)	A heated print head extrudes material and builds up model layer by layer.	Thermoplastics such as ABS and polylactic acid (PLA).	Can produce functional parts. Limited accuracy (+/- 0.1mm). Can produce parts 600 × 600 × 500mm. Machines are expensive. Can print in multiple colours.
Laminated object modelling (LOM)	Layers of material are cut to shape using a CNC laser or a knife and glued on top of one another.	Paper, metal foil or polymer sheet.	Less accurate than other methods. Surface finish can be poor. Difficult to produce hollow parts. Machines are relatively inexpensive. Materials are inexpensive.

Skill builder 14.2: Rapid prototype modelling

Rapid prototyping was developed as a means of modelling products during their development but it has become more common in the actual production of products.

Research and describe the advantages and disadvantages of using rapid prototyping as a means of manufacturing products.

Example answers on page 233

Applying your modelling skills

You will be assessed on your ability to apply modelling techniques to inform and communicate design decisions. Therefore you must make sure that you use appropriate models for a purpose. Remember there is a wide range of models, which can be used to:

- generate and explore ideas
- refine ideas
- communicate
- verify proposals.

The following pages show several different examples of appropriate uses of modelling.

In this example a student has used card sketch models to help generate initial ideas for a shelter. There are several examples of the use of sketch modelling on this page.

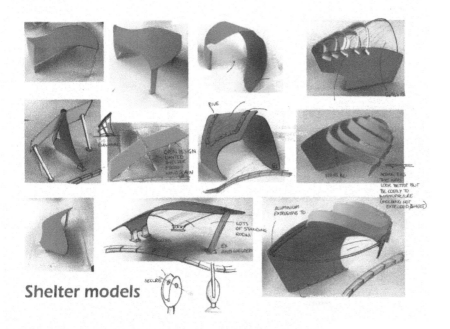

Shelter models

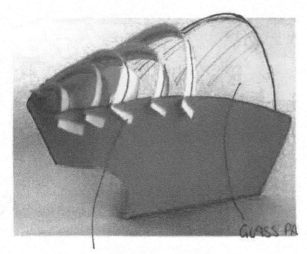

One advantage of sketch modelling is that it allows ideas to be communicated that may be difficult to sketch.

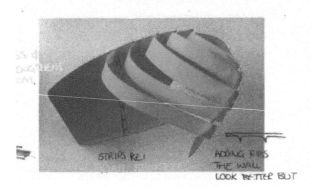

Sketch modelling also allows ideas to be viewed from any angle.

Another advantage of sketch modelling is that it can be used to very quickly identify possible issues and develop possible solutions.

On this model, the student has identified issues with fixing the shelter to the ground and fixing of the glass panel and has sketched possible solutions. They have also added annotations, which demonstrates their knowledge of assembly processes.

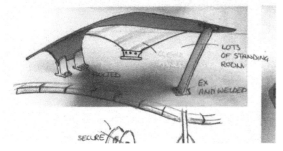

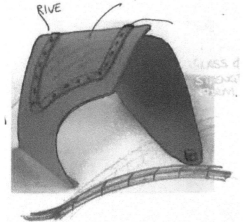

On this model, the student has developed the model slightly by considering possible materials and methods of strengthening the shelter. It should be noted that although these ideas may not be developed further, the information gained from them may be used on ideas actually taken forward.

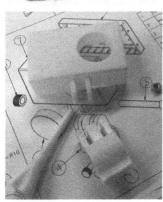
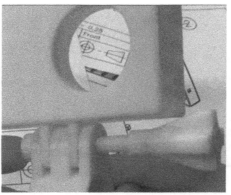
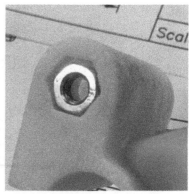

The example above shows a rapid prototype model to check that the parts of a camera mounting system fit together accurately.

In addition to this, the model was used to test whether the nut (a standard component) fitted into the recess created for it and also to explore aspects of ergonomics related to the assembly, adjustment and use of the mounting system.

This example shows two pages from a student's folio for the redesign of a tape measure to make it more comfortable. The original tape measure uses a number of standard components and these have to be used in the redesign. These standard components provide a starting point for the redesign. The redesign starts with examination and measurement of the standard components and a few initial sketches before moving onto modelling.

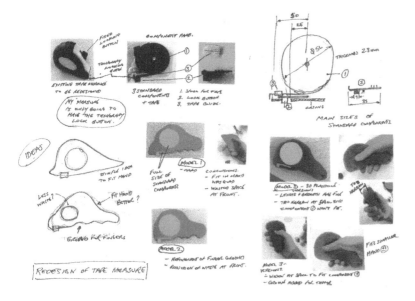

Scan to view folio work 1 and 2 on the Leckie resources page

The student used card sketch models to quickly check initial dimensions. Note that the fit of the standard components was checked at this stage and some adjustments were made. How well it fitted into a hand was also checked.

The student then made plasticine models to develop the form of the tape measure. This gave a better feel of the product and helped to develop its ergonomics with the introduction of grooves. The use of the standard components with this model also helped confirm sizes. Note that the student asked other people to test the size of the product.

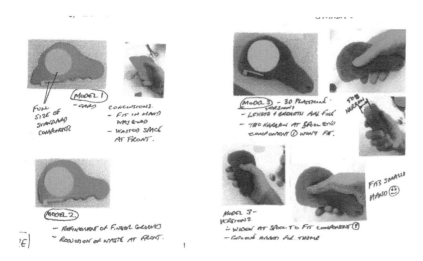

The student then modelled the tape measure with styrofoam to further develop the tape measure and present their proposal.

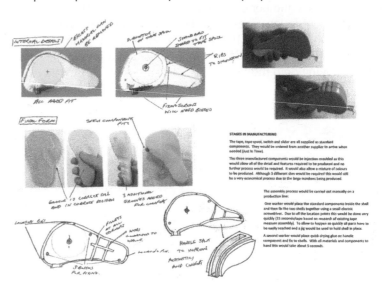

The styrofoam model very quickly highlighted a possible reduction in size, making it easier to handle and saving material. It also allowed the student to start considering how the product could be manufactured and they were able to start considering positions of features such as webs and bosses.

The styrofoam model also allowed further development of the form of the product and resulted in angled grooves on the underside of the handle.

The modelling at this stage was also used to develop the plan for commercial manufacture. Note that sketches and text were added to clarify detail.

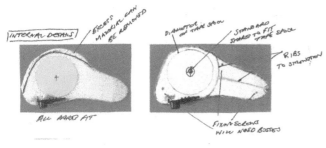

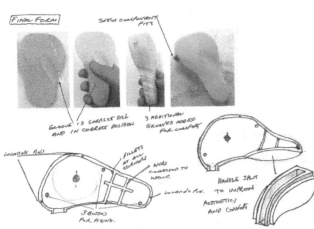

The final use of the styrofoam model was a presentation model. Note that the model shows detail such as split lines. Standard components have also been added to give a more realistic look.

Making styrofoam models

The student's folio for the tape measure shows a range of models made from different materials including card and plasticine. The presentation model was made from styrofoam. These show the stages of making the styrofoam model.

The front and side views of the tape measure were taken from a full size drawing and pasted onto a pre-cut block of styrofoam. Note that the block is bigger than required.

The block is now split for the two parts – it would be very difficult to do this after the block has been cut and shaped. The two parts are then fixed back together with double-sided tape.

The outline is now cut with a fret saw or band saw.

The block is reassembled using double-sided tape and the second face cut.

The body is then shaped using a range of files.

The body is smoothed using glass paper or wet and dry paper.

A white undercoat is applied and left to dry before being rubbed down with wet and dry paper. Two coats of acrylic paint were applied.

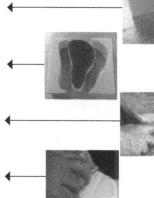

Producing a high quality finish on presentation models

Models that are used for presentations to clients can be finished to a very high standard with cellulose paint. The stages for this type of finish are as follows.

1. Take time and care to prepare the surface. All traces of the cutting and shaping stages should be removed using abrasive paper. All traces of surface dust should also be removed using a clean cloth.

2. Surfaces should be sealed before the primer is applied. This is done by brushing on a mixture of PVA and water (two parts PVA to one part water).

3. An appropriate spray primer can now be applied. The primer should be applied in thin coats, allowing each coat to dry before applying the next.

4. Once the final coat of primer has been applied the surfaces should be rubbed down using wet and dry paper and then wiped clean using a cloth and a spirit cleaner.

5. The paint should be applied in much the same way as the primer – using a number of thin coats. The surfaces should be rubbed down using wet and dry paper every two or three coats. This will ensure the paint goes on evenly and will reduce the risk of any runs. At this stage any runs would have to be smoothed out using wet and dry paper.

6. If the finished model has more than one final top colour, the lightest colour should always be applied first. These lighter areas will need to be masked off before the darker colour can be applied.

7. Once the desired finish has been reached the surfaces should be given one last going over with wet and dry paper before any final details or decals are added.

Care should be taken when applying cellulose paint. It should only be applied in well-ventilated areas with adequate extraction and filtration in place.

15. Protecting your ideas

Any piece of work that is the result of creative endeavour can be described as **intellectual property (IP)**. As with any property, intellectual property can be owned, sold, transferred or given away. Examples of intellectual property include software, inventions, trade secrets, formulas and brand names, as well as works of art and music.

Intellectual property rights (IPR) are the rights given to creator(s) of the property. These usually give the creator(s) an exclusive right over the use of the property for a certain period of time. It should be noted that, if you work for a company to develop the property, the rights are likely to belong to the company, not you.

There are several ways of protecting IPRs. The type of protection you can use depends on what you've created. It is possible, and often wise, to protect products by more than one method. Some types of protection are automatic and you have to apply for others.

Automatic protection

Type of protection	Examples of intellectual property
Copyright	Literary works, art, photography, films, TV, music, web content, sound recordings
Design right	Shapes of objects

You automatically get **copyright** protection when you create any of the properties in the table. You can mark your work with the copyright symbol (©), your name and the year of creation. It is useful to keep proof of the date of your copyright – this should be verified independently.

Copyright protection starts as soon as a work is created. The length of copyright depends on the type of work and can last for between 25–70 years after the creator's death. Once the copyright has expired, anyone can use or copy your work.

Design right only applies to the shape and configuration (how different parts of a design are arranged together) of objects.

Design right automatically protects your design for 10 years after it was first sold or 15 years after it was created, whichever is earliest. You can allow someone else to use your design by selling or giving them 'licence of right'. In the final five years you must supply a licence of right to anybody who asks.

Protection by application

Type of protection	Examples of intellectual property
Registered designs	Appearance of a product, e.g. shape, packaging, patterns.
Trademarks	Product names, logos, jingles.
Patents	Inventions and products, e.g. machines, tools, medicines.

Applying for these types of protection can take time, from one month for a registered design to five years for a patent. During this time you should keep your IP secret. If you need to show your idea to someone, get them to sign a non-disclosure agreement.

Registered design is used to protect the appearance or look of a product. The product must have individuality; it must not remind an informed person of an existing design. A registered design gives you the right to prevent others from using it for up to 25 years – you have to renew your design every five years.

Trademarks protect a symbol or sign, which may include words, pictures, logos or any combination of them. These symbols are often used to protect brands.

The ™ symbol is used for unregistered trade marks.

Once a trademark has been registered then the ® symbol can be used. A trademark in the UK can last forever, subject to a renewal being paid every 10 years.

Patents are used to protect new inventions, how they work, how they are made and what they are made from. It stops anyone else from making, importing, selling, or even using your invention without your permission. Once a patent has been applied for, then the term patent pending can be used. This allows you to discuss the idea openly without anyone else being able to use it. Once a patent has been granted, it gives protection for up to 20 years in the country where it was granted, as long as the annual renewal payments are made.

Patents are expensive and difficult to get, so you should check that this is the correct type of protection before you make an application. To be granted a patent, your invention must be something that can be made or used, is new and inventive – not just a simple modification.

SECTION 2:
Materials and Manufacturing

16. Materials

Selecting and justifying materials

Many different materials are available for the design and manufacture of products: plastics, metals, timber and composites. The selection of material(s) influences the functional, performance, aesthetic and ergonomic requirements of a product.

The choice of material places restrictions on the manufacturing processes. It is important that the most appropriate material is selected.

Selecting materials

The most suitable material(s) for a product is selected after consideration of the following factors:

- **Properties** of the material must be considered as these must be suited to the design requirements of the product.
- **Costs** of the materials must be considered as these must fall within budget. You should explore alternative materials with similar properties to ensure the most cost-effective solution is found.
- **Availability** of the materials must be considered as sourcing materials locally will help reduce transport costs and support the local economy.
- **Volume of production** must be considered as some materials may be more suitable for mass manufacturing.
- **Complexity of products or components** must be considered as they may require materials that can be easily formed or moulded.
- **Environmental issues** must be considered as the ability to recycle or reuse materials varies.
- **The performance requirements** must be considered as products will have different lifespans, be used in different conditions and require different levels of maintenance.

Material properties

You must be able to *select* materials that could be used to manufacture products and *justify* your choices. This requires a sound knowledge and understanding of the properties of a range of materials.

The following properties are identified as being important in determining the suitability of a particular material for a product or part of a product.

Acoustic	the ability to absorb and transfer sound
Chemical	how a material reacts to corrosion and chemicals
Electrical	how a material conducts or resists electrical currents
Optical	the ability to transmit and refract light
Physical	size, density, surface texture and aesthetic qualities should be considered
Thermal	the ability to transmit or resist the transfer of heat energy
Mechanical	how a material reacts to physical forces

Mechanical properties of materials include:

Strength	the ability of the material to withstand either tensile, compressive or shear force without permanently deforming or breaking
Toughness	the ability of the material to withstand sudden impact without fracturing
Brittleness	opposite of toughness; will break when subjected to sudden impact
Hardness	the ability to resist scratching, abrasion or wear
Stiffness	the ability of a material to resist deformation under an applied force
Elasticity	the ability of a material to return to its original size and shape on removal of an applied force
Ductility	the ability of a material to be deformed permanently by stretching, bending or twisting
Malleability	the ability of a material to be deformed by compressive forces without fracturing

Materials, such as metals or plastics, also have unique properties that inform selection decisions. These are detailed in the appropriate sections later in this book (for plastics see pages 124–127, for metals see pages 128–130 and for wood see pages 132–135).

Skill builder 16.1: Selecting and justifying materials

Select and justify the most important material requirements for each of the following products.

- bottle opener
- casing for hairdryers
- tennis racket frame
- bicycle frame

Example answers on page 234

Material selection and its impact on the environment and society

The extraction of metal ores, oils for plastics or the harvesting of timber can be damaging to the environment. In the current global market, the cost benefits of sourcing cheaper materials from developing countries, such as those in Asia or South America, must be weighed against the negative impact that this has on the environment.

Environmental damage is often further compounded by the pollution generated during the long journeys taken to transport the materials. For developing countries, however, supply of these materials provides an essential income.

Further information can be found on this on pages 192–197.

17. Plastics

Through their use of plastics, designers and manufacturers have changed the way we live today. Plastics have become commonplace in our society and their different properties are combined to produce a growing number of materials suitable for many different applications.

'Plastic' is a term used to describe any synthetic or organic polymer that can be formed or moulded into shape through the use of heat. Although most plastics are manufactured from petrochemicals, a growing number of organic plastics are being developed. These are manufactured from plant oils and have come about as a result of society's growing demand for 'greener' products.

Plastics can be split into two basic groups:

- thermoplastics
- thermoset plastics.

Thermoplastics are usually supplied in a granular form that needs to be heated prior to being formed in a mould.

The chemical makeup of thermoplastic allows it to be heated and cooled repeatedly without compromising the properties of the material; this means that any waste material can be recycled.

Examples of thermoplastics are acrylic, cellulose acetate, nylon, polycarbonate, polyethylene, polyvinyl chloride, polypropylene and polystyrene.

Thermoset plastics are typically produced by heating liquid or powder within a mould, allowing the material to cure into its hardened state. After it has hardened it cannot be heated and reshaped. Heating a thermoset too much after it has been cured will only result in charring and burning. Think about it like a boiled egg: once it has been hard boiled it cannot be softened. Thermoset plastics, however, have a number of advantages. Unlike thermoplastics, they retain their strength and shape even when heated. These plastics have excellent strength attributes (although they are brittle), and will not become weaker when subjected to high temperatures.

Examples of thermosets are epoxies, phenol, melamine and urea formaldehyde, along with a growing number of polyesters.

Thermosets are commonly combined with reinforcements, such as fibreglass, to form strong composites.

Designing with plastics

Good material selection involves matching the performances required from the product and the manufacturing process to the properties of the material. In order to do this, you must have a good understanding of the common properties of materials.

Additives, fillers and reinforcing fibres

A plastic may not have all the mechanical and physical properties required for a particular product and its manufacturing process. It may require additives to improve its mouldable properties, fillers to reduce its flexibility and reinforcements to alter its mechanical properties.

Additives

Additives are mixed with a plastic base material to make it last longer, be cleaner, safer, easier to process, or more colourful.

Additives cost money and increase the production costs. However, their inclusion can help the environment through the reduction in use of raw materials.

Common additives include: UV stabilisers, colourings, lubricants, plasticisers, antistatics, flame retardants and fungicides.

Fillers

Fillers are commonly added to plastics to reduce the amount of polymer required and, in most cases, also reduce the cost. However, there are a number of other advantages to adding a filler to a plastic, such as: increased material density, resulting in increased hardness and improvements in surface quality, increased stiffness and compressive strength, or decreased shrinkage.

Common fillers include: glass spheres, metal powder, silica sand, ceramic powder, mica flakes and sawdust.

Reinforcing fibres

Reinforcing fibres are commonplace in everyday plastic products and provide the same advantages as a filler, such as: increased tensile strength and improved impact strength.

However, health and safety concerns have been raised by some of the properties and fine nature of the fillers and fibres and these have resulted in increased processing costs.

Some fillers can also have an abrasive action on the manufacturing moulds, which reduces the lifespan of the mould.

Common reinforcing fibres include: glass fibre, carbon fibre, jute, nylon fibre and polyester fibre.

Plastic properties

Plastics are selected according to their properties to ensure they are suitable for the product's intended function, aesthetics, conditions of use, manufacturing and assembly processes. Properties that are important when selecting plastics (and are not described in the tables on pages 122–123) are shown below.

Density	the relationship between the weight and volume/size of the material
Shrinkage	the degree to which a material reduces in size, after forming
Transparency	a material's ability to transmit light
Plasticity	the ability to be easily shaped or moulded
Lubricity	the capacity for reducing friction

This table summarises some common plastics and their properties.

Plastic	Type	Properties	Commonly used in...
Epoxy resin (ER)	Thermoset	low shrinkage, strong, excellent adhesive qualities	surface coatings, encapsulation, lamination, bonding applications
Melamine formaldehyde (MF)		tasteless, waterproof, odourless, scratch resistant, electrical insulator	worktops, electrical insulation, buttons on clothing, tableware
Polyester resin (PR)		brittle, hard, stiff, electrical insulator, can be formed without heat or pressure	car body parts, hulls for boats
Urea formaldehyde (UF)		brittle, hard, stiff, electrical insulator, good adhesive qualities	electrical fittings, paper and textile coatings, wood adhesive
Acrylonitrile butadiene styrene (ABS)	Thermoplastic	chemical resistant, durable, strong, scratch resistant, high surface finish	cases for products, helmets, kitchenware, telephones
Cellulose acetate		flexible, hard, light, tough, transparent	containers, packaging, photographic film
Polyamide (PA) [Nylon]		durable, tough, easily machined, self-lubricating	bearings, bristles, clothing and upholstery (textiles), gears
Polyethylene (HDPE)		chemical resistant, tough	rigid: buckets, bowl, containers
Polyethylene (LDPE)		soft, pliable, electrical insulator	flexible: bags, bottles, sheathing for electrical cables, toys
Poly-methacrylate (PMMA) [Acrylic]		stiff, hard, clear, durable, easily machined and polished, easily scratched	cases, jewellery, reflectors and lenses for lights, signs
Polypropylene (PP)		chemical resistant, light, rigid, resistant to bending and fatigue	crates, seats, medical equipment, kitchen chopping boards, hinges
Polystyrene (PS)		buoyant, light, stiff, water resistant	containers, insulation, packaging, toys
Polyvinyl chloride (plasticised)		soft, flexible, electrical insulator	hosepipes, wire insulation
Polyvinyl chloride (uPVC)		abrasive resistant, rigid, water and weather resistant	bottles, guttering, pipes, window frames

18. Metals

There have been significant advances in our knowledge of metals and their properties and in our application of these materials in the thousands of years since the first metals were discovered.

Civilisation as we know it has evolved through the understanding of how to find, extract, form and alloy an increasing range of metals.

Metals, have allowed significant developments in agriculture, engineering, transport and electronics – all of which modern society relies upon.

Metals can be split into the following two groups: ferrous and non ferrous.

Ferrous metals, such as steel, contain iron and therefore need to be protected from corrosion caused by exposure to air and water. These metals can be protected using a variety of finishes, including special oil-based paints, electroplating processes such as galvanising, and plastic dip coating.

Ferrous metal alloys, such as mild steel, are relatively inexpensive and strong, making them suitable for large projects and structures like fencing, bridges and building frameworks.

Non-ferrous metals do not contain iron, therefore they are more resistant to corrosion and require less maintenance. Although non-ferrous metals do not rust, their appearance can change through exposure to the elements. Aluminium, for example, oxidises over time and loses its shine. Copper forms a green coating (verdigris), which can, in itself, be a desirable aesthetic on the right product, but can also be prevented with regular polishing if desired. These metals can be used without the need for protective finishes.

Plating can be used to improve the appearance and corrosion resistance of ferrous metals. Plating involves coating the ferrous metal in a non-ferrous metal such as zinc or chrome. This can be done by dip-coating or electroplating.

The chrome-plated shower head (right) benefits from the corrosion resistance, high lustre and natural appearance of the non-ferrous material.

Alloys

An alloy is formed by mixing two or more elements, of which at least one must be a metal. A binary alloy is formed when only two elements are mixed together.

Alloys tend to have metallic properties, although these will be different from those of the metal in the alloy. Let's take steel as an example.

Steel is a commonly used alloy, made from iron (metal) and carbon (non-metal). The resulting alloy (steel) is stronger than iron. There are many different steel alloys.

Varying the ratio of the carbon and iron or adding additional elements creates different types of steel. For example, chromium is added to make stainless steel, which is resistant to corrosion. Varying the ratio of carbon to iron alters the hardness of the steel.

Steel alloys have a wide range of applications including engineered structures, automotive parts and small domestic appliances. Altering the mixture of materials in an alloy can determine its ductility, strength, hardness and durability. Reasons for using an alloy may include needing a material with improved:

- strength-to-weight ratio
- corrosion resistance
- durability
- ductility
- strength in tension, compression or torsion.

Common alloys

Soft metals, such as copper, zinc, gold and aluminium, are often alloyed with other materials to make them suitable for a wider range of applications.

Aluminium is rarely used in its pure form, as it is too soft for structural applications. Duralumin, an aluminium alloy, has a better strength-to-weight ratio than aluminium and can be strengthened through heat treatment. It is used where good strength and machinability are required. Being malleable and light in weight makes it ideal for aircraft structures and engine parts. The addition of copper makes the Duralumin less resistant to corrosion than aluminium. Duralumin sheets are often coated in a layer of pure aluminium to combat corrosion.

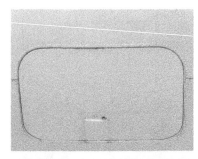

Alloy	Composition
Duralumin	94% aluminium 4% copper 0.5–1% manganese 0.5–1.5% magnesium
Brass	70% copper 30% zinc
Bronze	88% copper 12% tin
18ct gold	75% gold 15% silver 10% copper

Skill builder 18.1 Common metals

With a partner, create a set of material information cards which illustrate the range of uses and properties of the following metals:

- aluminium
- mild steel
- high carbon steel
- stainless steel
- zinc
- copper
- brass
- bronze
- cast iron.

Example answers on page 235

Designing with metals

Metals can shrink, spring back, distort and potentially defect as they are put under the stress and strain of forming processes. These factors should be considered when selecting metals for manufacturing.

Metals can be supplied in ingots for hot forming processes like casting; in solid blocks or rods for subtractive processes such as milling and turning; and in sheets for forming and fabricating.

Before you can select a metal that is suitable for the manufacturing processes you have in mind, and that suits the intended function of the product, you will need to have an understanding of:

- common metals, their properties and characteristics
- common processes and design limitations.

Metal properties

Metals are selected according to their properties to ensure they are suitable for the product's intended function, aesthetics, conditions of use, manufacturing and assembly processes. Properties that are important when selecting metals (and not described in the tables on pages 122–123) are shown below.

Conductivity	as well as conducting electricity, materials can conduct (or insulate) sound, light and heat
Corrosion resistance	materials with low resistance to corrosion require extra maintenance and a protective finish
Tensile strength	a measure of the force a material can withstand in compression (being squashed), tension (being stretched), torsion (being twisted) or shear (sideways pressure)
Melting point	may affect suitability for manufacturing process or function of the product

This table summarises some common metals and their properties.

Metal	Appearance	Properties	Melting point	Commonly used in...
Cast iron	dark grey	hard, brittle, strong in compression, weak in tension, self-lubricating, low resistance to corrosion	1535°C	machine tools, vices, engine blocks
Mild steel	dark grey	good tensile strength, tough, reasonably malleable, ductile, low resistance to corrosion	1350 – 1530°C	car bodies, girders
High carbon steel	grey	less ductile than mild steel, malleable and tougher than mild steel, can be hardened, then tempered by heat treatment, low resistance to corrosion	1353°C	cutting tools, drills, ball bearings
Stainless steel	silver grey	tough, ductile, higher tensile strength than mild steel, high resistance to corrosion	1400 – 1450°C	cutlery, kitchen sinks, door handles
Tin	silvery-white	soft, ductile and heavy, high resistance to corrosion	232°C	coating steel food cans, solder
Lead	bluish-gray	heavy, malleable and soft, high resistance to corrosion	327°C	roof flashing, batteries, radiation shielding
Aluminium	light silver	soft, ductile, malleable, good strength-to-weight ratio, lightweight, high resistance to corrosion	659°C	alloyed with other materials to make bike frames, aeroplane parts
Copper	orange	very good heat/electrical conductor, malleable, ductile, high resistance to corrosion	1083°C	electrical wires, heating pipes, pots
Brass	yellow gold	good heat/electrical conductor, harder than copper, high resistance to corrosion	927°C	decorative fittings
Bronze	brown	harder and tougher than brass, high resistance to corrosion	913°C	bearings, electrical conductors and springs
Zinc	bluish white	soft, ductile and malleable over 100°C, high resistance to corrosion	419°C	galvanising

19. Wood

Man has made use of wood for thousands of years as the primary material in construction and design.

Wood is an extremely useful natural material. It is nontoxic, biodegradeable and recyclable, while still offering the designer versatility, strength and cost effectiveness.

When grown sustainably, wood provides a far more environmentally friendly option than metals and plastics.

Wood is hard and fibrous in nature, made up of cells consisting of cellulose (natural resin) and lignin (the essential hard organic fibre).

Woods can be split into the following groups: **hardwoods, softwoods and manufactured boards** (timber derivatives).

The terms 'hardwood' and 'softwood' do not refer to the mechanical properties of the wood; some hardwoods can be soft and some softwoods can be hard.

Hardwoods, such as oak, mahogany, walnut and teak, are mostly produced from deciduous trees. Deciduous trees shed their leaves for part of the year. They have broad leaves that catch a lot of light and require a great amount of water. They can be found in warm climates such as Europe, New Zealand and Chile. Tropical hardwood trees can be found in Central and South America, Africa and Asia.

Hardwood trees are generally slow growing, taking around 100 years to become mature enough to harvest. This tends to make them harder and more expensive. Tropical hardwoods grow quicker and with greater height and girth, making them highly desirable. The destruction of the world's rainforests has led to deforestation and a resulting shortage of tropical hardwoods. More and more companies are looking to source hardwoods from sustainable sources such as purpose-grown forests and plantations.

Hardwoods are generally more attractive and durable than softwoods. They are commonly used in furniture and, to save on materials and cost, cheaper materials are often covered with thin layers of hardwood called veneers.

Softwoods, such as pine, cedar and spruce, are mostly produced from evergreen trees with needle-like leaves. They grow faster than hardwoods and in the cooler climates of Northern Europe, Scandinavia and Canada.

Since softwood trees grow faster than hardwood trees they can be purchased relatively cheaply and replaced more easily. Most softwood trees are ready for felling after around 30 years.

Softwoods are more open grained than hardwoods and tend to have knots, making them structurally weaker and less attractive. They are commonly used in construction and joinery work.

Manufactured boards are a man-made timber derivative often produced from the waste products of natural timber such as sawdust, bark and off-cuts. This waste product is normally bonded with resin, compressed and heated to form the board or sheet.

Manufactured board comes in a variety of forms dependent upon the base material.

- **Particleboards** such as chipboard are formed from sawdust and larger wood chips. They are compressed with adhesives to form stiff boards.
- **Fibreboards** such as MDF and hardboard are formed from binding fine dust or pulped wood fibres.
- **Layered veneered boards** such as plywood and blockboard use layers of thin veneers or strips of softwood between veneers. Cross-graining of layers ensures these plywood boards are stiff and strong.

Due to its availability in large sheets and relative ease of manufacture, manufactured board is commonly used for flat-pack furniture.

Advantages of using manufactured boards

- They are relatively inexpensive compared with natural timber and often make use of waste products.
- Manufactured boards tend to be very stable and less prone to warping or deforming than natural timber.
- They provide a smooth, even surface on which to apply a finish, such as paint or veneer.
- Being available in very large sheets (1220mm × 2240mm) makes them ideal for larger design projects.

Disadvantages of using manufactured boards

- The edges on particleboards or veneered fibreboards require 'facings'.
- They are difficult to maintain or repair, particularly when exposed to water.
- They lack the true wood appearance of natural timber, which makes them less desirable.

Designing with wood

Natural wood is a highly versatile material. It can be cut, drilled, shaped and even deliberately warped.

Natural wood is supplied in sawn boards of widths no greater than 300mm, although it is more commonly sourced at narrower widths. Wood laminated edge to edge has to be used to manufacture components wider than this. This has obvious implications for the cost and time taken to manufacture. Manufactured board should be considered for wider wooden parts.

A variety of methods can be used to assemble wooden components and various finishes used to enhance them. Different woods shrink and expand with changes in temperature so care must be taken when assembling dissimilar materials to allow for this.

Wood properties

Woods are selected according to their properties to ensure they are suitable for the product's intended function, aesthetics, conditions of use, manufacturing and assembly processes. Properties that are important when selecting wood (and not described in the tables on pages 122–123) are shown below.

Workability	how easily the wood can be worked with hand or machine tools and how suitable it is for gluing
Grain structure	the aesthetics of the grain; can also influence the strength of the cut wood
Source	where the wood was grown and harvested; designers have a responsibility to ensure this is sustainable
Finishing	how well the wood accepts finishes such as stain and polish

This table summarises some common woods and their properties.

Wood	Type	Properties	Commonly used in...
Oak	hardwood	strong, moderately durable, hard, tough, will stain steel	furniture, flooring, boat building, veneers
Mahogany		fairly strong, medium weight, easy to work, durable, prone to warping	available in long, wide boards, furniture, shop fittings, veneers
Beech		straight grained, strong, suitable for steam bending, tougher than oak	interior joinery, cabinet-making, turnery, bentwood furniture, veneers
Scots pine	softwood	straight grained but knotty, fairly strong, good workability	furniture, joinery, construction work
Red cedar		light, soft, weak, natural oils make it weather durable	exterior shingles, cladding, sheds
Spruce		non-durable, straight grained, light but strong, good elasticity	construction, interior joinery, aircraft and gliders, musical instruments
Plywood	manufactured board	stable, strong and easy to machine	furniture, joinery, construction work
Hardboard		cardboard-like, weak and brittle, smooth on one side, rough on the other	low cost furniture parts, e.g. cabinet backs, drawer bottoms
MDF (medium density fibreboard)		easily machined, moulded and painted	flat-pack furniture, suitable for painting or having a veneer applied
Chipboard		compressed wood chips, relatively weak and inexpensive	flat-pack furniture and suitable for having a veneer applied
Blockboard		stiff and heavy	furniture and worktops

20. Composites

Composites are formed by combining two or more materials with significantly different physical or chemical properties. The constituent materials in the resulting composite maintain their original properties and work together to produce a material with improved properties in comparison to the properties of the materials on their own.

Polymer composites

In polymer composites the constituent materials are known as the **matrix** and the **reinforcer**.

- The matrix material is normally a resin and is used to keep the reinforcer in place.
- The reinforcer is the fibres providing the structure or strength in the composite.

Let's look at an example. Fibreglass, also known as glass reinforced plastic (GRP), was one of the first composites and it was developed in the 1930s. It is a commonly used composite made from woven glass fibres set in a polymer resin. The flexible glass fibres can be woven in different directions which impacts the strength and weight of the GRP after the resin is added. The resin provides rigidity once it has cured (set). Typically, several layers of fibre glass and resin are added to increase the strength and rigidity of the GRP.

Fibreglass is strong, lightweight and easy to form, making it suitable for a wide range of applications, including boat hulls, exterior automotive parts and surfboards.

Bio-composites

Fibreglass

Resin

Research is ongoing to develop bio-composites, which use sustainable plant-based fibres and resins. In bio-composites, natural resins from trees or bio-resins made from plant oils are used as the matrix. Biofibres, such as coir (the mid-layer of coconut shells) and jute (vegetable fibres) are used as reinforcers. These bio-composites are 100% biodegradable.

Besides their relatively low cost, some of the main advantages of using composite materials are explained in the table below.

Advantage	Composition
High strength	Provides high-strength components. Composite materials can produce parts with specific mechanical properties, including impact resistance, compression resistance and tensile (or directional) strength with reinforcement in desired areas within a single part.
Lightweight	Better strength-to-weight ratio than most alloys.
Corrosion resistance and durability	Polymer composites do not rust or corrode as they have a high resistance to chemicals and environmental factors, resulting in long-lasting parts that require minimum maintenance.
Design flexibility and part consolidation	Composites can be fabricated into virtually any shape and size, and are suitable for concept and production parts. The design and fabrication of composites is extremely flexible. This allows individual complex parts to be produced, which can replace complex assemblies that would require numerous components if using traditional materials.
Dimensional stability	Composites maintain their shape and functionality, even under severe mechanical and environmental stresses.

21. Manufacturing processes

Many different processes are available for the design and manufacture of products. It is important that the most appropriate process is selected.

Selecting processes

The most suitable processes for components are selected after consideration of the following factors:

- **Volume of production** must be considered as some processes are only suitable/economically viable for mass manufacturing.
- **Size of components** must be considered as some processes are better suited to small components.
- **Speed of production** must be considered as processes range from manual to fully automated. This impacts the time and cost to manufacture each component.
- **Tooling costs** of the process must be considered to ensure they fall within budget. The designer should explore alternative processes that can produce parts with similar characteristics to ensure the most cost-effective solution is found.
- **Accuracy** of the part must be considered as some processes are unsuitable for creating parts with a high level of dimensional accuracy.
- **Surface quality** must be considered as quality varies depending on the process. Few processes are able to produce a quality finish with a high level of surface detail.
- **Materials** must be considered as many processes are restricted to wood, metal or plastics only. The process selected must be suitable to use with the material with the required properties.
- **Environmental issues** must be considered as designers and manufacturers have a responsibility to minimise negative impact on the environment and society. Recycling waste from subtractive or finishing processes may also have economic benefits.

Manufacturing processing can be categorised as follows:

Machining is a subtractive process that removes material. Processes include turning, milling, drilling, tapping, routering and spindle moulding.

Moulding is a forming process where material is added and formed in a mould or formed by compression forces. Processes include gravity die casting, pressure die casting, investment casting, sand casting, extrusion, compression moulding, injection moulding, blow moulding and rotational moulding.

Sheet material processes can be altered using a range of processes that form or cut the material.

- Forming processes, such as roll forming, spinning, bending, deep drawing, press forming, line bending and vacuum forming.
- Cutting processes such as punching, blanking and shearing.

In the question paper and during all design work, there is a requirement to select suitable manufacturing processes for the product in question. Categorising the processes can help you to rule out the unsuitable processes. For example, the sink top shown here is made from a sheet metal. Therefore the moulding and machining processes could be ruled out. The table below summarises some of the key points of common manufacturing processes for woods (**W**), metals (**M**) and plastics (**P**).

MACHINING	Volume	Size	Speed	Tooling cost	Accuracy	Surface quality	W/M/P
Milling	Mid to high	•●⬤	High	Low	High	High	W/M/P
Turning*	Low to high	•●⬤	Low	Low	Mid to high	Mid to high	W/M
Spindle moulding*	Low to high	•●⬤	High	Low	Mid	Mid	W
Routering*	Low to high	•●⬤	High	Low	Mid	Mid	W
Drilling*	Low to high	•●⬤	Mid	Low	Low to mid	Mid	W/M/P

MOULDING	Volume	Size	Speed	Tooling cost	Accuracy	Surface quality	W/M/P
Pressure die casting	High	•●⬤	High	High	High	High	M/P
Gravity die casting	Mid	●⬤	Mid	Mid	Mid	High	P
Investment casting	Mid to high	•●⬤	Low	High	High	High	M
Sand casting*	Low to mid	•●⬤	Low	Low	Low	Low	M
Extrusion	Low to high	●⬤	Low	Low	Mid	High	M/P
Drop forging	Low to high	•●⬤	High	High	Low	Low	M
Injection moulding	High	•●	High	High	High	High	M/P
Compression moulding	Mid	•●⬤	Mid	Mid	High	High	P
Blow moulding	High	•●	High	High	Mid to high	High	P
Rotational moulding	Low to high	•●⬤	Low	Low	Mid	High	P

SHEET PROCESSES	Volume	Size	Speed	Tooling cost	Accuracy	Surface quality	W/M/P
Folding*	Low to high	•●⬤	Low to high	Low	Mid	High	M
Roll forming*	High	●⬤	Mid	Mid to high	High	High	M
Spinning*	Low to high	•●⬤	Low	Mid	Mid to high	Mid to high	M
Press forming*	Low to high	•●⬤	High	Mid to high	High	High	M
Piercing/blanking*	Mid	•●⬤	Mid	Mid	Mid	Mid	M
Line bending*	Low to high	•●⬤	High	Low	Mid	Mid	P
Vacuum forming*	Low to high	•●⬤	Mid	Low to mid	Mid	Mid	P

*These processes may be manual, semi-automated or fully CNC.

●●⬤ refers to the suitability for small, medium and large components.
Volume relates to production systems (see pages 184–191).

22. Machining processes: Turning

Machining is the name given to processes that cut away from solid metal. These include drilling, boring, turning and milling.

Turning metal

The two main parts of the dart shown below have been turned on a lathe.

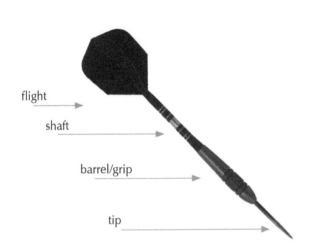

flight

shaft

barrel/grip

tip

The shaft and barrel can be made from a range of metals including tungsten and brass. Tungsten is denser, allowing thinner barrels to be turned, which permits tighter clusters of darts on the dart board. The greater the percentage of tungsten, the more expensive the dart.

All dart barrels start as an extruded rod. The barrel is **centre drilled** and **bored**, before being **tapered**, and then **threaded** at one end. Taper turning involves reducing the diameter of the rod gradually, creating a cone-shaped feature. This helps make the dart more aerodynamic. Threading allows the dart shaft to be screwed onto the end of the shaft when the finished components are being assembled. The barrels are turned on a metal lathe using a range of processes to create the form and texture of the finished component. The rod is **parallel turned** to reduce the diameter of the bar where required. The grip on a dart varies by design. Special tools on the lathe are used to create the desired grooves, which allow the player to have good grip. Typical grip patterns are shown below.

Knurling is a process that presses detail or pattern onto the revolving workpiece. ID/part numbers can also be applied using specialist marking tools in the knurling process. Once the detail is complete, the barrel is **parted off** from the rod to allow the remaining processes to be carried out.

The shafts shown on the two darts are made from aluminium, which is relatively lightweight and can be anodised, allowing the shafts to be dyed different colours.

The dart shaft is turned and threaded from extruded aluminium using similar turning processes. Further machining is required to cut the slots for the flights on the end of the shaft.

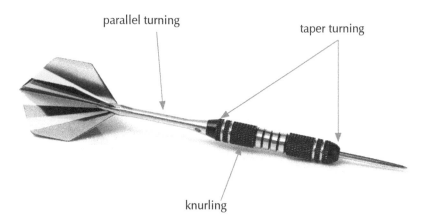

parallel turning

taper turning

knurling

A steel tip is pressed into the hole in the barrel. A push fit is a secure and economical way to assemble the components as the dart is not exposed to any tension, which would pull the components apart during use. The other end of the barrel is then screwed into the shaft before the flights are inserted into the slots.

Most darts are manufactured using Computer Numeric ally Controlled (CNC) lathes. Despite the initial high set-up costs there are numerous advantages to CNC:

- continual production as machines don't require comfort and other breaks
- increased production rate as machines work faster
- greater accuracy of repetition
- more highly complex parts can be made
- reduction in waste as a result of human error.

A typical dart can be machined and assembled in just under a minute using CNC technology.

Skill builder 22.1: Turning

Metal turning is a machining process. A cooling oil or other fluid is required to stop the metal and tools from heating up too much. Waste material, known as swarf, is created during the turning process.

1. Discuss the impact the turning process may have on the environment.

The dart shown has been machined using turning and boring processes.

2. Sketch a range of different dart shafts and barrels in good proportion. Annotate them to clarify key machining features, such as knurling, parallel turning, taper turning, threading and boring.

Example answers on page 236

Turning key points

- Machining process
- CNC or manual
- Cutting process
- High quality finish
- Revolved profile

23. Machining processes: Routering

Routering (or routing) is one of the most commonly used and versatile processes for shaping wood.

The guitar body shown below has been manufactured using routering.

Interchangeable bits, or cutters, are secured in the router, then driven by a motor at very high speeds (typically 20 000–30 000 revolutions per minute). The router is pressed into and moved through the wood, removing material as it goes. The profiles of the edges and grooves are dependent upon the shape of the cutter used to create them.

The high speeds at which the router operates ensure the cutting process is performed quickly and leaves a high quality finish.

Routering can either be performed manually or, for larger volumes of manufacturing, using CNC (computer numerical control).

CNC routering

CNC routers are machines that vary in size, ranging from table top machines to ones with large work areas capable of holding a full sheet of manufactured board.

CNC routering is used extensively in the manufacture of flat-pack furniture. The raw material, normally manufactured board, is fixed down and the router moves over and into it to cut out the components.

The flat form of flat-pack furniture components clearly suits sheet material and can quickly and accurately be cut. Complex details such as joints or holes for any knock down fittings can also be created by the router (with different cutters selected).

Components are created in CAD then translated into a path for the CNC router to follow. Software can be used to suggest the optimum layout for components on a sheet to minimise the amount of waste material.

Manual routering

Manual routering is performed using a power router, such as the one shown below. It can be performed in one of two ways:

- The operator fixes the material and runs the router over it manually to perform cutting.
- Alternatively, a router table can be used. The router is fixed, upside down underneath the table with the cutter projecting through the table top. This speeds up the process when making a batch of similar components.

Skill builder 23.1: Routering

Generate ideas for an occasional table that could be manufactured using routering and manufactured board.

The table should have no more than five parts. All joins should be designed into the individual components. No other components can be used for joining.

Example answers on page 237

24: Moulding processes: Sand casting

The rocking horse ornament (left) has been manufactured from cast brass. There are different methods of casting, all with advantages and disadvantages. The Design and Manufacture course requires an understanding of:

- sand casting
- investment casting
- die casting.

These processes all involve pouring molten metal into a cavity and allowing it to cool and harden.

Sand casting is the simplest and the most labour intensive of the casting processes. A low-cost **pattern** is used to create a mould cavity. A special moulding sand is packed around the pattern. When the pattern is removed, the sand holds its shape.

Two channels are dug out to allow the molten metal to be poured in and excess gasses and metal to rise out.

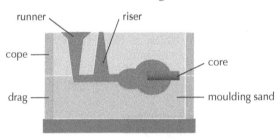

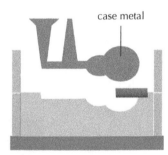

As the horse has been sand cast, the initial surface finish is rough and requires additional finishing processes. The excess metal from the runner and riser and evidence of split lines also have to be removed. This finishing process is known as fettling.

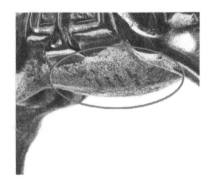

The final surface quality depends on the grade of sand used during the casting. Air bubbles or contamination of the molten raw material will reduce the surface quality of the cast part. This will determine the level of machining that takes place to finish the casting. Some pitting is evident in the surface of the rocking horse as shown here.

There are a number of reasons sand casting may be selected:

- hollow items can be produced using sand cores
- low initial investment to set up
- suitable for low production runs
- large components can be produced (up to 1 tonne)
- suitable for ferrous and non-ferrous metals.

It should be noted that sand casting can be labour intensive, which leads to a high unit cost. It is not suitable for creating thin sections or for mass production.

Investment casting is more expensive than sand casting and is usually only used when sand casting isn't suitable, such as when dimensional accuracy, thin wall sections and good surface detail are required. Although both ferrous and non-ferrous metals can be investment cast, the process cannot be used to produce items as large as those made by sand casting.

Patterns in investment casting are normally made of wax. These wax patterns are assembled onto a sprue before being repeatedly dipped into a ceramic mixture and covered in a sand mixture to create an outer shell. The mould is preheated to allow the wax to be removed before pouring in the molten metal. When the metal has cooled, the outer shell is chipped away, leaving parts with a high surface finish and a level of detail that matches the original wax patterns.

There are a number of reasons sand casting may be selected:

- complex designs are possible as there are no draft requirements
- repeated accuracy is consistent
- small tolerances may be achieved
- minimal finishing processes required
- low tooling costs.

Skill builder 24.1: Casting

These barbell weights were sand cast.

1. Explain why sand casting is a suitable process for manufacturing the weights.

Many parts of this turbojet engine have been investment cast.

2. Explain why investment casting is a suitable process for the turbo engine parts.

Example answers on page 237

25. Moulding processes: Die casting

Die casting is a suitable process for the manufacture of the toy car shown below because it can produce a high volume of complex parts with a high level of accuracy.

There are two common types of die casting.

- **Gravity die casting** is commonly used for mid volume production runs and creates high quality castings with limited accuracy and minimum wall thickness of 3–5mm.
- **High-pressure die casting** is used for high volume production runs and creates parts with fine surface detail and walls as little as 1mm thick.

Both methods involve the use of a furnace, molten metal, die-casting machine, and die (reusable mould). Like most die-cast products, the toy car is made from a non-ferrous metal, such as **aluminium** or **zinc alloys**, which is melted in the furnace and then injected into the die in the die-casting machine. The machine can vary depending on the materials being cast. **Hot chamber machines** are used for metals with low melting points, such as zinc alloys, and **cold chamber machines** are used for metals with higher melting points, such as aluminium alloys. Regardless of machine type, after the molten metal is injected into the die, it rapidly cools and solidifies forming the final part, called the **casting**.

The following features should be considered when designing for die casting.

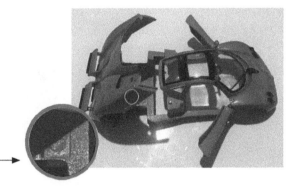

ejection point ⟶

Parting lines/split lines and ejection points

A die-cast component always has a split line, also referred to as a parting line. This is where the different parts of the die come together, forming a closed mould. A trace of this line is often visible on the component. See the example of split lines on injection moulding on page 158.

If the die wears or parts are incorrectly positioned, molten metal will seep through the gap, leaving excess material (flash) along the parting line. An example of flash on injection moulding is shown on page 158. Ejection points will also be visible on the part (see above). The small circles left on the inside of the car were created by the ejector pins, which pushed the part from the mould.

Additional processes to remove split lines incur costs. Split lines and ejection marks should be placed strategically to minimise costs and to preserve aesthetics.

Split lines should be kept as flat and straight as possible to allow easy separation of the die.

Drafts

The **draft** is the taper on a die. The purpose of the draft is to make it easier to remove the casting from the die. The metal used, shape of the wall, and depth of the die will all influence the angle of the draft required.

Die-cast parts are prone to shrinkage when they cool in the die. To ensure the parts are easy to remove, the internal draft should be larger than the draft on the outer walls. Any untapped holes also require a draft to compensate for shrinkage.

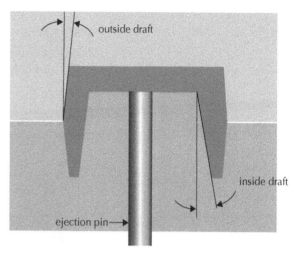

Undercuts

An **undercut** is a recessed feature that would prevent the mould from being pulled away in the parting direction. This could be an internal recess or pocket. Die-cast parts are often complex and undercuts are common.

Undercuts should not be positioned in the direction of the sliding cores.

Sliding cores are added to the design of the tooling. These slide into position during the casting process to create the undercut features on the die-cast part then they slide out for the ejection process.

external undercut

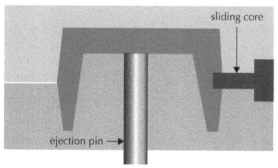

internal undercut

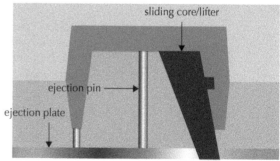

The sliding core is pulled out before the main parts of the die are separated. The ejection pins are then used to release the metal.

In this example the upper part of the die would be lifted off first. The ejector pins would then push the casting and lifter out of the die. Finally, the metal part would be separated from the lifter.

Fillets

A fillet is a curved transition at an edge or a corner. Fillets are used to reduce sudden changes in direction in the part.

Sharp edges and corners can cause problems during the casting process; trapped air and hard to reach cavities can lead to incomplete castings. Incorporating fillets in the design is necessary to enhance the flow of molten metal into the die cavity.

Fillets can be added nearly anywhere on a component to avoid sharp edges and corners, but cannot be used at the split line.

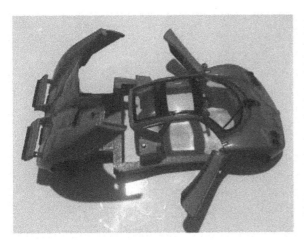 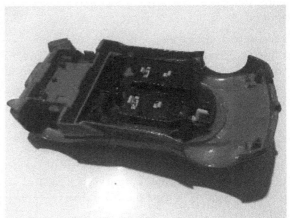

Wall thickness

Uniform wall thickness means consistency in thickness of material across the die-cast part.

Uniform wall thickness is not essential but will produce a higher quality component. Fillets and gradual changes of thickness can reduce the likelihood of defects.

Sudden changes in wall thickness (in fact any abrupt changes in the geometry of the component) will interfere with the flow of molten metal into the cavity. This can result in warping and defects in the surface finish. A wall thickness of as little as 0.2mm can be achieved.

Ribs

Ribs are thin-walled protrusions that can be added to parts to increase their strength and stiffness.

Ribs are of benefit as they increase the strength of the product without increasing the overall weight or wall thickness. Ribs also provide additional gateways to allow the molten material to flow to parts of the die that are more difficult to fill.

Ribs should be filleted and should be offset to reduce the stress spreading across the part.

Bosses

Bosses are cylindrical protrusions on a component that are used as mounting points for screws, fasteners and other components.

As bosses are narrow features, it is difficult for the molten metal to flow into them. Including hollow bosses in the die reduces the need for additional machining and processes.

Bosses should be hollow to maintain uniform wall thickness.

Adding fillets, draft angles and ribs can reduce the chance of manufacturing defects by improving the access of the molten metal to the boss, and making the component easier to remove from the die.

For more information on bosses see page 160.

Features of die casting

- Injection points
- Ejection marks
- Split lines
- Flash
- Bosses
- Ribs
- Webs
- Fillets
- Draft angle
- Openings
- Undercuts
- Surface detail
- High quality finish

without fillets

with fillets

Openings

Die-cast parts are often complex housings or enclosures. Frequently there are windows, openings or holes in the part that may be required to house other components, like the windscreens in the die-cast toy car body.

Additional features, such as overflows, bridges and crossfeeders can be used to channel and maintain the flow of metal and prevent unwanted casting within the holes.

Draft angles should be added to these openings to ease removal, by preventing the part from gripping to the die.

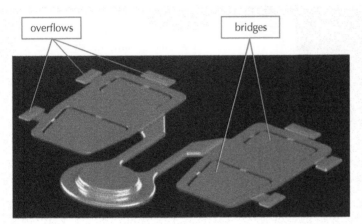
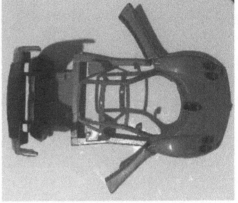

Surface detail

Brand names, product logos or fine detail can be included in the mould design of die-cast products.

A raised symbol will not normally complicate the die-casting process. However, it will use additional molten metal. The die-cast car has surface detail including the headlights, registration plates and handle details.

Recessing surface detail uses less material, thereby reducing production costs.

Raised surface detail uses additional material and increases production costs.

Skill builder 25.1: Die-cast food mixer

The food mixer is made largely from a zinc alloy.

1. Explain why this is a suitable material for the die-casting process.

2. Explain why die casting is a suitable process for manufacturing the casing of the food mixer.

Example answers on page 237

Skill builder 25.2: Die-casting features

The following features are considered when designing the body casing for any die-cast part.

- Fillets
- Ribs
- Bosses
- Split lines
- Ejection marks
- Wall thickness
- Draft

A concept for a new alloy wheel is shown below. Use a series of annotated sketches of an alloy wheel to show how each feature could be incorporated to ensure good mould design.

Example answers on page 238

26. Moulding processes: Extrusion moulding

Extrusion moulding

Extrusion moulding is commonly used in the production of UPVC window and door frames. This process allows the production of continuous lengths with a uniform section and can be used to produce products in a range of materials. A wide range of plastics is commonly used and metals, such as aluminium, copper and magnesium, can also be extruded.

The initial product produced by the process is seldom used without additional processing or forming. In most cases, the product is cut up into manageable lengths before being joined, formed or assembled into a finished product.

The initial process is fairly simple and can be described as like squeezing toothpaste from a tube. The material (metal or plastic) is pushed through a shaped die and is then cooled, using either air or water, on exiting the die.

Visual features of extrusion moulding

There are a number of visual clues that allow the process to be identified:

- uniform profile (cross section)
- complex form (inside and out)
- straight lengths joined at the corners
- dual density materials can be formed together.

The complex internal detailing is used to add strength, while keeping material costs and weight down. This contrasts with the simplistic outer form of the window frame.

The photos show the complex internal detail of the frame and the simple way in which the long lengths are mitred and glued at the corners to form the frame. The red part is a steel inner core, which is used to stop the frame warping.

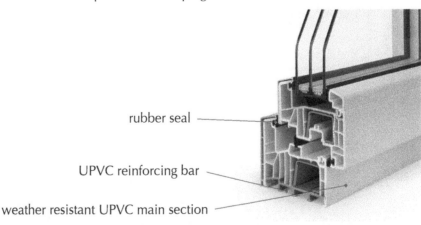

rubber seal

UPVC reinforcing bar

weather resistant UPVC main section

Designing for manufacture

When designing products that are to be extruded, there are eight main points to consider.

1.	When designing rigid products, try to keep wall thicknesses uniform, as varying the wall thicknesses will result in different cooling rates and may lead to distortion.	
2.	Aim to keep any internal detailing within hollow sections to a minimum. Holding the die in place during the moulding process is very difficult and often requires opening the outer profile during the forming process.	
3.	Hollow sections within the outer profiles should also be avoided due to the difficulties involved in holding the inner hollow in place.	
4.	If any internal features, such as webs, grooves or snap fittings, are to be included, try to allow for good access to these features.	
5.	Although clear plastic profiles can be achieved, these are only possible with some materials. When good optical clarity is a priority, use polycarbonate or PETG for the best results. If cost is the overall determining factor, rigid PVC should be used.	
6.	Dual density extrusions are achieved by combining both rigid and flexible materials. Two machines are needed to feed the two different materials through the same die, allowing rigid profiles to have flexible lips or for two rigid profiles to be joined by a flexible hinge.	
7.	Several colours can be combined in one extrusion.	
8.	When designing flexible profiles using elastomers, all the previous rules apply except that variable wall thicknesses can be achieved.	Thin / Thick

Extrusion (metal)

Extrusions can be solid, hollow or open as shown below. Dies to produce these example extrusions are also shown.

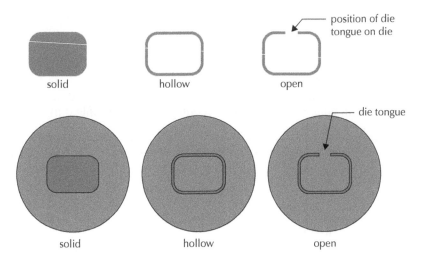

Selecting the correct die angle and speed of extrusion can prevent common defects in an extruded part. Centre cracking, surface breakage and piping defects often occur.

Centre cracking occurs as the metal at the outer edge flows more quickly than the metal in the centre. If the difference is too great, stress occurs in the metal, resulting in cracking.

Surface breakage occurs when there is too much friction from the die, causing the outer metal to stick to it. This creates stress in the material as it is pushed through the die, causing the outer extrusion to crack.

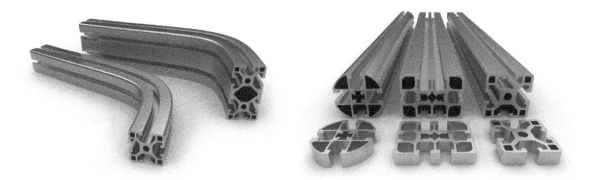

To reduce the chance of defects:

- symmetry is preferred in all extruded parts
- where parts are hollow or open a uniform wall thickness should be used; where this isn't possible radii should be used to avoid sudden changes in wall thickness
- where parts are open, the die tongue (shown in the diagram above right) should be centred with rounded edges to reduce wear on the die.

Skill builder 26.1: Designing for extrusion moulding

The children's garden seats shown here have been made from wood. The manufacturer is considering having them redesigned so that they can be made from recycled plastic.

- Explain why the seats may be better manufactured from extruded lengths of plastic, rather than from individually moulded component parts.
- State a suitable plastic for manufacturing the seats and justify your answer.

Example answers on page 238

Skill builder 26.2: Extrusion

Redesign the following parts to make them suitable for metal extrusion.

Sketch your solutions in 2D and 3D using a range of graphic techniques, such as two-point perspective, isometric, oblique and orthographic.

Example answers on page 239

27. Drop forging

The golf club heads shown have been manufactured by **drop forging** carbon steel.

Forging can produce stronger parts than alternative processes, like casting. Forged parts, such as the golf club head, are formed by compressing the metal. As the metal is compressed, gaps in the metal are closed and the molecular structure of the metal changes, strengthening the part.

Drop forging requires a force exceeding 2000 tonnes to form the metal. The forging can take place with hot or cold metal, depending on the final properties required.

- **Hot forging** – greater deformation is possible, giving increased ductility of material.
- **Cold forging** – greater force is required to forge, leading to a better surface finish and accuracy of part.

There are two types of drop forging – **open-die** and **closed-die**.

Open-die forging requires an operator to place the work-piece under the die. The die forges the metal without fully enclosing the work-piece, as shown below.

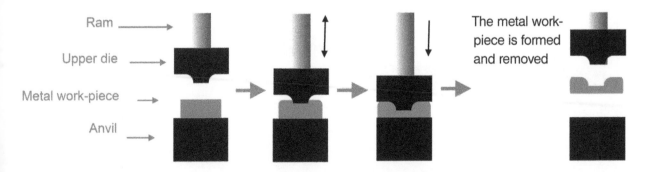

Closed-die forging compresses the work-piece between an upper and lower die, fully enclosing the work-piece. The top die is attached to the ram. This ram impacts the work-piece several times until the material deforms to fill the cavity between the dies. This can result in flash where excess metal flows between the dies, as shown in the diagram below.

| The metal work-piece is placed onto the lowed die | The ram presses the upper die down onto the metal, repeatedly | Flash may be visible when the forged part is removed. |

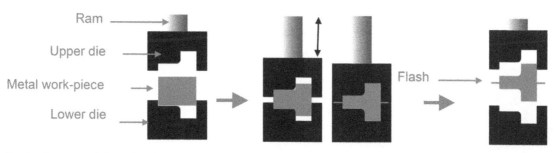

Ram
Upper die
Metal work-piece
Lower die
Flash

For both types of drop forging:

- high strength parts are created through grain orientation
- parting lines should be on a single plane or follow the contour of the part
- draft between 3° and 7° should be applied
- fillets and radii should be used.

Skill builder 27.1: Forging

1. Explain why drop forging is a suitable process for manufacturing the G-cramp.
2. Describe how the threaded hole may have been created.
3. Sketch the G-cramp shown, or use one from your class. Annotate and comment on the following:
   - fillets
   - split lines
   - ribs
   - surface finish.

Example answers on page 239

28. Moulding processes: Injection moulding

Various parts of the remote control shown have been manufactured using the injection moulding process.

Visual features of injection moulding

- Highly complex, accurate parts with good surface finishes.
- Visible injection point and ejection marks.
- Visible signs of flashing.

This photo shows the complex nature of the bottom half of the case. There are a number of surfaces that need to locate in position to allow the top and bottom halves of the case to fit together. The four circular marks on either side of the photo are the ejection marks. These marks are caused by the ejector pins that are used to push the case from the mould at the end of the mould cycle – remember, plastics contract or shrink on cooling, often causing the product to become stuck onto the mould.

One of the injection points or 'sprue pin' marks can be clearly seen in this photo. This is the mark left at the place where the molten plastic is injected into the mould cavity. There is often more than one injection point, allowing the plastic to flow through the mould to completely fill the cavity. Designers and manufacturers put a lot of thought into where these points are placed.

The injector and ejector pins are carefully placed so that their marks do not spoil the aesthetics of the product.

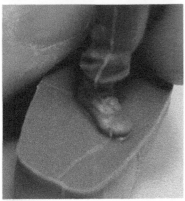

Flash is an excess of plastic along the join line of the mould, caused by a combination of incorrect moulding pressure and/or worn or damaged moulds. There were no signs of flash on the remote control casing but the close-up of the base of the toy soldier here shows obvious signs of flash along the split line of the mould.

Designing for manufacture

There are many different issues that must be considered when designing plastic products to make them suitable for injection moulding.

Wall thickness

The overall wall thickness of a product is the result of a fine balance between the functional performance of the product and the capabilities of the manufacturing process.

When designing parts that will be injection moulded, the wall thickness that can be achieved depends on the type of plastic used:

- **pure plastics** should be 0.5mm to 5mm
- **filled** or reinforced plastics should be 0.75mm to 3mm.

All plastics are susceptible to shrinkage; the amount and rate of shrinkage is affected by the volume of plastic and the wall thickness. To avoid any irregular shrinkage and distortion, wall thicknesses should be kept as uniform as possible.

Avoid sharp transitions

There is often a need to change the wall thickness due to functional or aesthetic reasons. When this is the case, take care to avoid sharp transitions from one thickness to another. The use of gradual transitions reduces the likelihood of warping or distortion in the finished product.

Radius corners

Sharp edges are not ideal when designing plastic products. Some plastics tend to be notch sensitive, resulting in chipping and deforming on external corners. Sharp internal corners create stresses, bringing in an increased likelihood of cracking.

The simplest way to avoid this is to create radius corners, which:

- reduce the internal stresses, and avoid cracks and fractures
- reduce the likelihood of damage to the external corners
- allow the plastic to flow freely around the mould
- allow the part to be removed from the mould easily.

There are a number of guidelines that should be observed when designing radius corners:

- internal corners should have a radius of between 0.5–0.75 times the wall thickness
- external radius should be equal to the internal radius plus the wall thickness.

Strengthening

Ribs, or webs, are a good way to introduce strength to specific parts of a product without having to increase the overall wall thickness. Ribs are also often used to provide support or locate the internal parts of a product, such as holding a spring, button or printed circuit board in place.

web/rib

boss

The size, shape and position of the rib very much depends on the stress the part is likely to experience. The guidelines for designing ribs are as follows:

- ribs should be 50–75% of the overall wall thickness of the main part
- the depth of a rib should be no more than five times its thickness
- ribs should have tapered sides to reduce the risk of the component sticking in the mould
- a number of smaller ribs are better that one large one.

It is often necessary to have ribs running in different directions and care must be taken where they cross or meet. It is important to maintain a uniform thicknesses along the rib, to reduce the risk of distortion. Areas where ribs cross need a hollow boss placed at the intersection to help maintain a uniform wall thickness.

Boss placed at the intersection of two webs

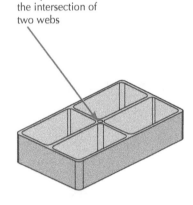

Bosses

Bosses are used to aid in the assembly of injection-moulded parts. They can also be used to align or locate different component parts. Care should be taken when positioning bosses as they can cause stress and distortion of the part being moulded.

Guidelines for designing bosses are:

- all bosses should be tapered to reduce the risk of becoming stuck in the mould
- radius corners should be placed at the base of the boss, as this reduces the stress in the corner
- ideally, bosses should be attached to the outer wall by a rib
- when being designed to accommodate a screw, the depth and diameter of the hole must be able to accommodate the length of the screw.

Draft angles

Throughout the design of the product, take care to ensure that ribs and bosses have tapered sides to allow them to be removed from the mould at the end of the moulding cycle.

The same care must to be taken with the overall form of the product. A 1° taper should be applied to all of the external surfaces to allow the product to be removed from the mould with the minimum of force, using ejector pins built into the mould.

The picture shows a cut-away through the bottom half of the remote control case. The draft angle was over 1° and a large radius was applied to the corner, but there was still a need for an ejector pin to be used on the back surface.

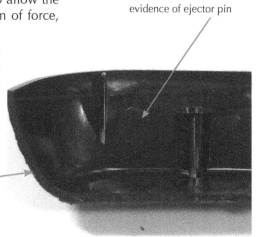

evidence of ejector pin

draft angle and large radius

Skill builder 28.1: Designing for injection moulding

A graphic of a poorly designed calculator case is shown. No consideration has been given to the materials to be used or the manufacturing process to be used in its production.

- Select a suitable plastic for the design of the calculator case. Remember to consider the performance of the calculator case and the properties of the material when making your selection.

- Redesign the calculator case so that it can be manufactured successfully using injection moulding. Present your solution using appropriate graphic techniques.

Example answers on page 240

29. Moulding processes: Compression moulding

The electrical socket shown was manufactured from a thermoset plastic using compression moulding. The process allows a range of products to be manufactured, from small detailed parts like electrical sockets to large-scale, solid plastic car bumpers. Larger products tend to have thicker walls and can be manufactured more economically using compression moulding rather than injection moulding, largely due to the reduced cost of the tooling.

The process itself is fairly simple and, in most cases, makes use of a two-part heated mould. The two parts come together to compress a measured amount of thermoset plastic, usually in the form of granules, putty-like billets or preforms. The moulding pressure is then maintained until the material has cooled before the mould is split and the product removed.

The main body of the electrical socket shown above was manufactured from phenol-formaldehyde using compression moulding. There are a number of visual clues that allow the process to be identified:

- complex shape
- a variety of wall thicknesses
- noticeable draft angle
- good surface finish
- no undercuts
- signs of flash.

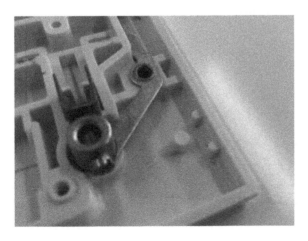

The complex form of both the main body and back plate, draft angles, internal radiused corners, webs and bosses can be clearly seen in the photos above.

Note: the cut edge of the front plate has been coloured red to illustrate the complex nature of the form and the variety of wall thicknesses.

Designing for manufacture

When designing products that are to be compression moulded, the designer can incorporate many of the same features that are present in injection moulding, such as:

- bosses
- ribs and webs
- draft angles
- radiused corners.

When these features are present, the guidance issued for injection moulding should be followed (see pages 158–161).

There are a number of additional considerations to address if the compression moulding process is to run smoothly.

- **Calculating the correct amount of material**
  This will reduce the amount of waste and the risk of the plastic not filling the mould cavity. The use of CAD software in the design of the product allows designers to accurately calculate the volume of material required.

- **Balancing the time and energy required to heat the material**
  Balancing the heating time and the energy requirements can reduce the moulding cycle time while also keeping running costs down.

- **Calculating the required moulding force**
  Obtaining the correct moulding force is vital if the product is to be formed correctly. Too much force and flashing will occur; too little and the product will not be fully formed.

- **Incorporating a cooling system into the mould**
  Cooling the mould quickly reduces the moulding cycle time, cutting costs and increasing productivity.

Skill builder 29.1: Designing for compression moulding

The design considerations for injection moulding and compression moulding share some common features.

Identify a product that has been compression moulded and explain why this process was used rather than injection moulding.

Example answers on page 241

---

30. Moulding processes: Injection blow moulding

The water bottles and petrol can shown below have been manufactured using two different types of blow moulding, known as **extrusion blow moulding** and **injection blow moulding**. Blow moulding is used to produce hollow containers. Although these processes are different, both products share the same basic features.

Features of blow moulding

- Hollow containers.
- Simplistic forms.
- No interior detailing.
- Limited possibilities for altering wall thicknesses.

Designing for manufacture

When designing for blow moulding the following should be considered:

- Wall thicknesses should be kept as uniform as possible, this will reduce the moulding cycle time, speeding up production.
- Moulds should be kept as symmetrical as possible, reducing the risk of distortion.
- Draft angle should be at 90° to the direction that the mould opens.
- Larger radii work better – avoid sharp corners where possible.

Injection blow moulding

All products manufactured using injection blow moulding start off with the manufacture of an injection moulded parison which, in the case of the bottle, resembles a test tube with a threaded top. The use of the preformed parison allows the bottle to have a rigid, highly detailed screw top, this level of detail could not be produced using extrusion blow moulding.

The parison is preheated prior to being enclosed within the final mould.

Once the mould is closed, hot air is pumped into the parison, causing it to expand and fill the mould cavity. The air pressure is maintained until the plastic has cooled sufficiently, allowing it to be removed from the mould.

During the moulding process the area around the screw thread is kept cool by circulating cooling fluid inside the mould; this allows the detailed thread to retain its shape.

Visual features of injection blow moulding

The water bottle was manufactured from PET using the injection blow moulding process.

There are a number of features that allow this process to be identified.

- Highly detailed and accurate screw threaded top.
- Evidence of a sprue pin mark on the bottom of the bottle.
- Evidence of split lines along the line of symmetry of the bottle.
- Very thin wall thicknesses.

These are common features found on blow moulded bottles of this type. The wall thicknesses can be 0.1mm in some cases and because the PET has been stretched its strength is increased, resulting in a lightweight bottle capable of holding carbonated drinks without their forms distorting due to internal pressures.

Skill builder 30.1: Designing for injection blow moulding

The graphic below shows a poorly designed 500ml shampoo bottle.

- Select a suitable plastic for the design of the shampoo bottle. Remember to consider the basic requirements of the bottle and the properties of the material when making your selection.
- Redesign the bottle so that it can be successfully manufactured using injection blow moulding.

Present your solution using appropriate graphic techniques and consider the following in response to the task:

- radius the corners
- draft angles
- position of the sprue.

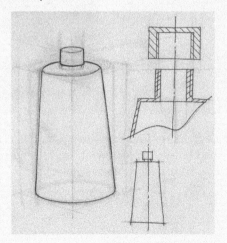

Example answers on page 242

31. Moulding processes: Extrusion blow moulding

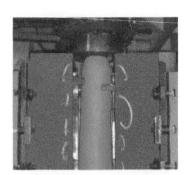

Extrusion blow moulding is the simplest and least expensive form of blow moulding, and is suitable for short production runs. The process allows a wide variety of finished container forms with wide neck openings and the ability to mould handles into the finished container.

The process itself is very simple: a plasticised tube of polymer material is lowered from an extruder and enclosed within a water-cooled mould.

Air is then pumped through the neck of the container, causing the plastic to expand and fill the mould cavity. The air pressure is maintained until the plastic has cooled sufficiently, allowing it to be removed from the mould.

Once the mould has opened, any excess material can be trimmed off and this waste recycled.

Visual features of extrusion blow moulding

The petrol can was manufactured from high-density polyethylene (HDPE) using the extrusion blow moulding process. There are a number of features that allow this process to be identified:

- simplistic, chunky screw threads
- evidence of shearing of excess materials along the top and bottom of the can
- handles moulded into the form of the container
- solid sections within the container.

These are common features found on blow moulded containers of this type. The wall thicknesses can be much thicker than injection blow moulded products, as thick as 6mm in some cases.

Extrusion blow moulding allows for the inclusion of solid sections within the containers, the petrol can was cut in half along the line of symmetry (where the two halves of the mould would have met). The top left of the photo shows a solid section – this was created by tightly pressing the two halves of the material together leaving no cavity for any air to be pumped into.

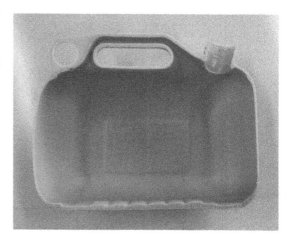

Inconsistencies in the wall thickness around the handle and along the bottom of the container can also be seen. This is a result of the difficulty in controlling how much the plastic stretches and should be considered when using the extrusion blow moulding process.

All extrusion blow moulded parts will require excess material to be removed. Trimming excess material can prove difficult in some cases and designers need to think carefully about this as secondary processes increase production costs.

Skill builder 31.1: Designing for extrusion blow moulding

The graphic below shows an initial idea for a 5-litre oil container. No consideration has been given to the materials to be used or the manufacturing process used in its production.

- Select a suitable plastic for the design of the container, remembering to consider basic requirements of the bottle and the properties of the material when making your selection.

- Redesign the container so that it can be successfully manufactured using extrusion blow moulding. Present your solution using appropriate graphic techniques.

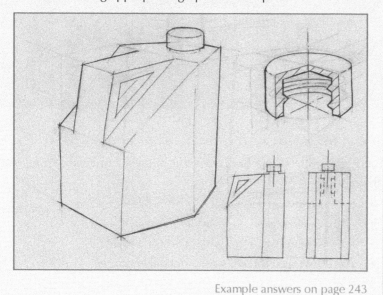

Example answers on page 243

32. Moulding processes: Rotational moulding

All of the products shown have been produced using rotational moulding. Rotational moulding produces hollow products from powdered resin, rather than from sheet or granules, and is the simplest of the moulding processes. It is unique in that it does not apply a force to the material during the mould cycle. The material is heated to its plastic state inside the mould and then the mould rotates, allowing the material to flow within and fill the mould cavity.

The process is used in the production of a range of products, from large fluid tanks and children's outdoor play items, to small-scale toys and engine parts.

Polyethylene (HDPE and LDPE) is currently used in the manufacture of over 80% of rotationally moulded products. Other materials used include:

- nylon
- polycarbonate (PC)
- polyester (PES)
- polypropylene (PP)
- polyvinyl chloride (PVC).

Visual features of rotational moulding

There are a number of visual clues that allow the process of rotational moulding to be identified:

- high quality surface finish
- slight draw angles
- hollow, simplistic form with good surface detail
- consistent wall thicknesses with thicker corners.

Designing for manufacture

When designing for rotational moulding, the following points should be considered carefully:

- **Materials and tooling costs**

  Compared to other plastic-moulding processes, the production costs for rotational moulds are relatively low and there is seldom a need for secondary processing. As a result, the process can be suited to short production runs.

  Wall thickness and product weight can be easily controlled by altering the amount of material placed within the mould; it's not uncommon for the finished wall thickness to come within a tolerance of ±10%. There is little or no wastage, reducing the material cost.

  The material thickness and volume of material both influence the length of the mould cycle.

- **Size, scale and detail**

  Products of almost any size can be rotationally moulded; the only limiting factor is the size of the available oven.

  Totally enclosed hollow products with intricate contours and undercuts can be moulded, as well as products with openings.

  Rotational moulding is capable of producing products with an excellent finish and complex surface detail, and plastic or metal inserts can be placed within the mould to become integral parts of the product, increasing strength and improving functionality.

Skill builder 32.1: Designing for rotational moulding

The kayak below was rotationally moulded. Explain why this is a suitable process.

Example answers on page 244

33. Sheet processes: Metal

This cafetiere has been manufactured using a range of processes. Once the plunger has been disassembled, it is easy to see the different components and their individual forms.

The round discs are produced using a range of **shearing processes**.

- **Blanking** has been used to cut out the round discs from a sheet of material. In blanking, the piece that is cut out of the sheet becomes the blank. The sheet that is left after the blanks have been cut (the waste) can be melted down and recycled. The machine can produce numerous blanks in one operation.

blanking 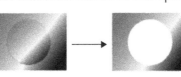 waste blank

- **Piercing** has been used to punch out the shaped holes from the blank. Piercing is one of many punching processes, such as notching, slitting and slotting, that are used to remove material as scrap. The holes are all punched out simultaneously, meaning faster processing and reduced cost. During the piercing process, the material that is punched out is the waste material.

piercing 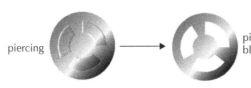 pierced blank  waste

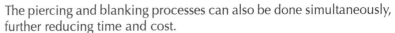

The piercing and blanking processes can also be done simultaneously, further reducing time and cost.

Both of these processes require a press that uses shearing force, causing the metal to fail then separate, resulting in a cut. Shear marks can be seen on the components. These generally appear as diagonal lines on the cut edge of the metal. As the force is deforming the metal, it creates a burr on the edge where the metal fractures as the die punches through.

After the piercing is complete, the parts are formed. Forming sheet metal involves modifying the geometry, rather than removing any material.

Press forming

The components of the cafetiere have been formed using the press forming process. This process is also used to produce mild-steel car body panels and stainless steel kitchen sinks.

Press-formed parts have radius bends and curves, as shown in the cafetiere components. These prevent the metal from fracturing. Press-formed parts can vary from simple 2D curves to complex shell-like structures such as car body panels, which are strong with a good surface finish.

The depth of the curve required on the cafetiere component is shallow, allowing the form to be created in one press. When deeper forms are required, deep drawing is used.

Deep drawing is used when the intended depth of the part is greater than half the diameter of the part. Kitchen sinks require deep drawing.

A hydraulic press is used to form the part in stages, as shown in the diagram below. This allows the metal to stretch bit by bit. This process requires a different die for each stage, increasing the time taken and cost to produce a part.

Stages of deep drawing

 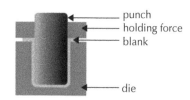

— punch
— holding force
— blank

— die

Skill builder 33.1: Fabricating sheet metal

The following processes are used when fabricating sheet metal.

With a partner, carry out research into the following processes. Using small pieces of card, model each of the processes. You should label them and mount them onto an A3 sheet.

- Notching
- Blanking
- Nibbling

- Slotting
- Spinning
- Folding

- Piercing
- Rolling

Example answers on page 244

34. Sheet processes: Spinning

The shade on the fisherman's lamp (left) has been manufactured by spinning sheet copper. Spinning is sometimes known as spin forming.

Copper is suitable for spinning as it is malleable. Copper also has an appealing aesthetic, making it desirable for decorative products. A circular metal disc (the blank) is clamped onto a mandrel and turned at high speed. A roller tool is then used to form the spinning metal over the mandrel, as shown below.

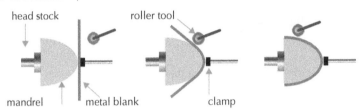

The spinning process produces thin-walled items from sheet metal that are symmetrical across a central axis. Common forms are shown on the left.

 hemispherical

 venturi

cone

dished

stepped

 flanged

Spinning the component has advantages over other processes. Spinning:

- wastes little material as the work-piece is cut to size with minimal trimming required
- can be made thinner than is possible with alternative processes, meaning more efficient use of material
- uses tooling that is less expensive than that required for casting or press-forming processes
- can be made in low or high production runs, manually or by fully automated processes
- costs less to produce, due to: reduced material, less waste and cheaper tooling
- is seamless
- is formed at room temperature, with cold working strengthening the material.

Spun products generally undergo additional processes for finishing or to produce more complex parts.

A spun product can be identified by its form and often by the concentric

lines that appear around the surface of the component, as shown in the photo (left). Other products that are produced by spinning include woks, decorative household goods, urns and large satellite dishes.

Materials that can be spun

- carbon steel
- aluminium
- brass
- copper
- bronze
- titanium

35. Sheet processes: Vacuum forming

Vacuum forming is commonly used in the production of a wide range of plastic products, such as large car roof boxes and bathtubs, down to small-scale plastic food containers, packaging and disposable plastic cups. The vacuum forming process is the simplest and least expensive of all of the plastic forming processes and is the one that is most likely to be available in schools.

The process allows for the production of a range of products with fairly simplistic forms that are moulded from sheet plastic.

Thermoplastics such as polystyrene are commonly used in the vacuum forming process.

The finished product has to have additional processing, such as removal of excess material.

On a small scale, the process itself is very simple, only requiring a sheet of thermoplastic to be heated and drawn down onto the pattern using a vacuum. Once the plastic has cooled, it can be removed from the pattern and the excess material trimmed off.

The process requires little investment, other than the initial cost of the machine. Because the pressures used to help form the plastic sheet are so low, patterns can be manufactured from wood, aluminium or other low-cost materials, and can be inexpensive and quick to produce.

Visual features of vacuum forming

There are a number of visual clues that allow the process to be identified:

- thin wall thicknesses (10mm maximum)
- large draw angles
- simplistic forms
- inconsistences in wall thicknesses.

The plastic cups shown on the previous page look simple, but on closer inspection they have all the characteristic features of a vacuum-formed product that has been cleverly designed to benefit the user, while ensuring a cost effective, quick and simple moulding cycle.

The cups were mass produced in a large batch from a thin sheet of polypropylene measuring 1m x 1m. A sheet this size will have enabled 100 cups to be manufactured in a single cycle, before the individual cups are cut from the sheet and the safety edge on the top rolled over in another process.

The photos below clearly show the simplistic form of the cup, alongside the detail of the safety edge and the thinning of the material at the corner of the cup.

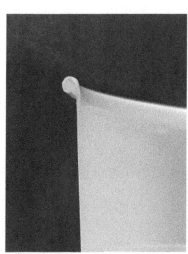
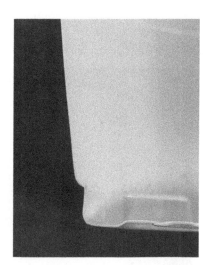

Designing for manufacture

When designing products that are to be vacuum formed, the designer should consider the following:

- **Male or female pattern**
  Deciding whether to use a male or female pattern influences the finish and form, and where thinning occurs.

- **Draft angle**
  Large draft angles, as much as 5°, must be worked into the design to allow the product to be removed from the pattern. Thin wall thicknesses can cause excessive shrinkage, resulting in the product being difficult to remove from the pattern.

- **Sharp changes in direction**
  Sharp changes in direction should be avoided as this causes thinning of the material as it stretches around the pattern. Radiusing the corners helps to reduce this thinning.

- **Simplicity of the form**
  Keeping the form of the product simple, minimising detail and avoiding undercuts reduces the need for additional post-production processing, in turn reducing the production costs.

Skill builder 35.1: Designing for vacuum forming

Vacuum-formed packaging is required for the peeler shown.

- Select a suitable plastic for the design of the potato peeler's packaging. Remember to consider the function of the packaging and the properties of the material when making your selection.

- Design the potato peeler packaging so that it can be successfully manufactured using vacuum forming. Present your solution using appropriate graphic techniques.

Example answers on page 245

36. Joining materials

Most products that consist of more than one component part will feature some kind of joining method. The designer must have knowledge and understanding of joining methods in order to select the most appropriate method for the parts being joined.

Selecting the most appropriate joining method

When exploring methods of joining parts, consideration should be given to the following:

- **What materials are being joined together?**
  Certain methods are only suitable for specific materials. Joining of dissimilar materials can be problematic as they may have different properties, such as their reaction to temperature change or different surface textures.

- **Should the join be permanent or non-permanent?**
  Some joins need to be permanent enough to prevent the product being separated for safety reasons or to maintain its performance. Some products, such as flat-pack furniture, should be able to be disassembled and reassembled.

- **What are the performance requirements of the join?**
  The functional requirements of the product and the environment in which it will be used will influence the joining methods. For example, will the join have to create a watertight seal when exposed to water or chemicals?

The types of joining methods used will also affect the aesthetics and cost of the product.

A table of common joining methods and their suitability for different materials is shown opposite.

Skill builder 36.1: Selecting joining methods

Select a product that you are familiar with that can be taken apart.

Identify and justify the types of joining methods used. Try to be specific.

Example answers on page 246

Common methods of joining materials

Joining method	Permanent or non-permanent?	Key points	Plastic to plastic	Plastic to metal	Plastic to wood	Metal to metal	Metal to wood	Wood to wood
Polyvinyl acetate (PVA)	Permanent	Strong, can be water-resistant, non-staining wood glue.						✓
Contact adhesive	Permanent	Very quick setting, used for bonding different materials.	✓	✓	✓	✓	✓	✓
Epoxy resin	Permanent	It is used to form a rigid bond with dissimilar materials, with the exception of silicon rubber.	✓	✓	✓	✓	✓	✓
Liquid cements	Permanent	A range of liquid cements (including Tensol and Polystyrene) for joining thermoplastics.	✓					
Superglue (Cyanoacrylate)	Permanent	Best used on small surface areas. Useful for prototype modelling. Creates a strong, water-resistant join.	✓	✓	✓	✓	✓	✓
Welding	Permanent	See pages 178–179.				✓		
Soldering and Brazing	Permanent	Allows the joining of dissimilar metals. Use of lower temperatures reduces warping and heat damage.				✓		
Riveting	Semi-permanent	Mechanical fastener that comes in a range of materials and head types. Suitable for joining different types of sheet materials.	✓	✓	✓	✓	✓	✓
Wood joints	Non-permanent or permanent	Can be used with adhesive to make permanent.						✓
Nuts and bolts	Non-permanent	Come in a variety of materials and forms.	✓	✓	✓	✓	✓	✓
Screws	Non-permanent	Come in a variety of materials and forms.	✓	✓	✓	✓	✓	✓
Knock-down fittings	Non-permanent	See page 180.		✓	✓	✓	✓	

CASE STUDY

The dining chair shown here has been manufactured using a range of processes and different types of steel.

The backrest is made from three main parts: a fabric cover, foam padding and a frame made from extruded mild steel. The frame is shown below, with some of the foam removed. Mild steel is suitable for the frame as it is ductile, has good weld ability and is relatively low cost. Although mild steel corrodes, this will be minimal under normal conditions of use and should not affect the performance or aesthetics of the chair during its expected usable life. A small amount of rust is visible next to the welds in the image of the backrest below right.

Welding is an **inexpensive process** for permanently joining the frame components. As the frame is fully covered, no unnecessary processes have been used to clean up the bead produced by the weld.

Welding is also used to join parts of the base. Here (below left) additional machining has taken place to smooth out the welds where the joint is visible, making the extruded leg appear as one part.

There are various types of welding. The metals being joined, its melting point and thickness will determine the type of welding process that can be used.

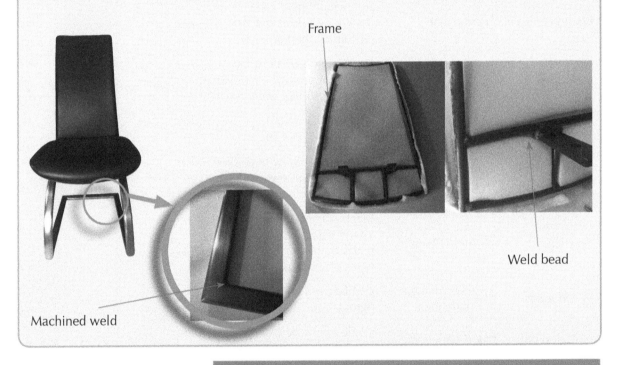

Frame

Weld bead

Machined weld

Skill builder 36.2: Welding

The following processes are used to weld metal.

- MIG welding
- TIG welding
- SPOT/resistance welding
- STICK/SMAW welding

With a partner, carry out research into these welding processes. Create a fact sheet for each of the processes and show the common weld joints produced by each one.

Example answers on pages 247 and 248

The table below can be used as a quick reference guide to selecting a suitable welding process.

Weld type	Key points	Steel	Stainless steel	Aluminium	Copper	Brass	Cast iron
MIG	Consumable wire electrode spool, semi-automatic process, less skill required than TIG, suitable for long welds and produces uniform weld bead.	✓	✓	✓			
TIG	Non-consumable electrodes, can be used with or without filler rods. Produces slag free, high quality welds and is suitable for thin materials.	✓	✓	✓	✓	✓	
SPOT	Non consumable electrodes, suitable for thin materials. Produces slag free welds and requires a low level of skill.	✓	✓				
STICK/SMAW	Uses consumable electrodes and is best suited for short welds. Inexpensive and portable, and finish varies with skill.	✓	✓	✓			✓

Let's now go back to our analysis of the materials and manufacture of the dining chair, to consider the stand part of the chair. As the chair stand will be seen, it has been made from stainless steel. Although more expensive than mild steel, stainless steel has better resistance to corrosion and does not require additional protective finishes.

The chair frames are manufactured from round, oval, rectangular and u-shape extrusions (see pages 152–154). These can be manufactured or supplied in standard sizes, then cut to length, formed, machined and joined as required. This would be more cost effective than having custom parts supplied, shaped or cut to size.

Bolts are used to assemble the seat to the frame. These are easy to locate due to the holes in the flat surface of the joining extrusions. Washers are used with the bolts to even out the pressure when the bolt is tightened. They also prevent the bolt loosening and damage to the frame.

Polypropylene plastic caps are used to seal the end of the extruded frame. These caps join to the chair using a simple push fit. The purpose of the caps is to protect the end of the extrusion and improve the overall aesthetic of the chair.

Knock-down fittings

Knock-down fittings provide a method of joining wooden parts together using minimal skill and basic equipment. Often, only a screwdriver or allen key is required. Often these are included with self-assembly products for convenience.

Using knock-down fittings allows manufacturers to package products in an unassembled state. This reduces the storage space required by manufacturers and retailers and also allows for easier transportation for consumers and manufacturers. These 'flat-packed' products save companies money, meaning they can offer consumers products at a lower price.

There are several different types of knock-down fittings available. When selecting the most appropriate type to use, the following should be considered:

- the materials being joined, whether natural wood or manufactured board
- how strong a join is required.

Types of knock-down fitting

Here are some common knock-down fittings.

	CAM locks		Metal brackets/plates
	SCAN fittings		FIXIT blocks
	LOK joint		Wooden battens or buttons

Adhesives

Adhesives are used to bond two materials together. This bond is normally permanent. The type of adhesive used is usually determined by the materials to be joined, however, the performance requirements of the product can also influence this choice.

PVA (polyvinyl acetate) glue

This is a particularly useful adhesive for gluing porous materials, making it suitable for wood. It provides a flexible and strong bond. It can also be used to seal MDF edges prior to painting. Light cramping can be required, which can make awkward components difficult to join.

Contact adhesives

These are most commonly used to bond plastic laminates to manufactured boards. The adhesive is applied to the two materials being joined and left to dry. The materials are then placed together. When the adhesive on each piece comes into contact a bond is created instantly and the materials cannot be adjusted. This negates any need for cramping.

Epoxy resin

This adhesive comes in two parts – a resin and a hardener. Both are mixed together prior to application. This causes a chemical reaction, which sets the adhesive. Epoxies are commonly used to join dissimilar materials. They provide a strong and rigid join. Not suitable for silicon rubber.

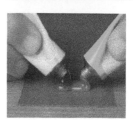

Liquid solvent cements

These are commonly used for joining thermoplastics. When applied to a plastic surface a chemical reaction takes place allowing a bond to occur. A larger gluing area will ensure a stronger bond.

Superglue (cyanoacrylate)

These adhesives create a fast acting, strong and waterproof join. However, their uses are limited to smaller surface areas. This makes them useful when assembling small or early models, less so for functional prototypes.

37. Finishing materials

Finishing materials

It is common for materials to have a finish applied prior to or during manufacture. Applying a suitable finish can help increase the aesthetic appeal of a material whilst helping to maintain its lifespan.

You must be able to identify and justify finishing processes used during the manufacture of products. You must also be able to apply this knowledge in the design of your own products.

The type of finish applied will primarily depend upon the material being finished.

Finishing wood

Sawn wood is porous and will absorb liquids, which may cause damage to it. Applying a finish to wood helps to seal it and protect it from the environment or any other potentially damaging materials it may come into contact with.

Finishing wood normally requires preparation by planing then sanding through increasing grades of abrasive paper. Imperfections will often be filled.

Some wood, such as that used in construction, may already be treated with preserver prior to purchase. This provides protection against insects and decay.

Finishing metal

Similar to wood, applying a finish to metals may change their appearance and offer increased protection from corrosion.

In particular, ferrous metals (page 128), if left unfinished, will rust when exposed to oxygen or moisture. It is therefore essential that a suitable finish is considered during the design of products that feature these materials.

As metals tend to be excellent conductors of electricity and heat, many processes, such as anodising and galvanising, take advantage of this to apply the finish.

Finishing plastic

Plastic is known as a *self-finishing* material. The properties of most plastics make them very resistant to corrosion. Processes such as injection moulding require little extra finishing work to the plastic component. This obviously reduces the number of stages during manufacture and helps to reduce costs.

Plastics will accept some finishes and, sometimes, it may be necessary to alter the appearance of the plastic post manufacture. See the table on the opposite page.

Common finishes

A list of common finishes is shown below.

Finish	Material	Description
Paints	Wood, metal or, less commonly, plastic	Available as oil, solvent or water-based. Provides a coloured, opaque finish. Can be used for interior or exterior purposes.
Varnishes	Wood	Transparent finish that highlights and protects the surface below. Can be used for interior or exterior purposes. Normally requires several coats.
Stain	Wood	Soaked up by wood to provide a darkened or coloured finish. Some stains have preservative qualities. Some varnishes include stain. Can be used for interior or exterior purposes.
Wax	Wood	A transparent finish that can be buffed to a high gloss. Normally used after other finishes such as polish or lacquer.
Oil	Wood or metal	Slower to dry than water-based finishes. Enhances the appearance of grain on wood. Oils include Danish, linseed and teak. Can also be used to protect metal from rust.
Preserver	Wood	For exterior use. Transparent finish that provides wood with protection from rot and insect damage.
Polishes	Wood, metal or plastic	Traditional finish for interior furniture. Includes shellac and wax polishes. Wax is normally applied afterwards to further refine the finish.
Plastic dip coating	Metal	Metal is heated and dipped into thermoplastic powder. Smooth, continuous, coloured and opaque finish. Protects the metal from the environment and rust.
Powder coating	Most commonly metal but also wood and plastic	Applied to metal electrostatically (powder is positively charged then sprayed at the grounded material). Provides a continuous, smooth, coloured and opaque finish. Improved corrosion protection and reduced waste compared to paint.
Anodising	Metal	Used on aluminium to provide a protective, corrosion-resistant layer. Involves electrolysis and acid baths. Can allow the aluminium to be dyed or improve its adhesion.
Galvanising	Metal	Used to coat iron or steel with a protective layer of zinc.
Electroplating	Metal	Used to coat metal with chromium, silver or another metal using electrolysis.

38. Planning and production systems

Companies use a variety of different methods to monitor and plan the progress of the design and manufacture of products, the most common of which are Gantt charts and flowcharts.

Gantt charts

Gantt charts are used to plan specific tasks against time. They allow members of a team to see what time is available for each given task, what sequence the tasks have to be completed in and also which tasks can be completed at the same time.

Planning projects in this way allows managers to keep track of progress through a project and also helps the team keep within budget.

Periods of high activity or cost, where most strain is placed on a workforce or manufacturing facility, can be identified easily and appropriate measures put in place, helping to reduce the risk of failure.

The Gantt chart below shows how a company has split up the time between January and June into six four-week blocks to allow them to plan a sequence of 10 tasks.

	January				February				March				April				May				June			
Week No.	1	2	3	4	5	6	7	8	9	10	11	12	13	14	15	16	17	18	19	20	21	22	23	24
Task 1																								
Task 2																								
Task 3																								
Task 4																								
Task 5																								
Task 6																								
Task 7																								
Task 8																								
Task 9																								
Task 10																								

Skill builder 38.1: Gantt charts

Study the Gantt chart above and answer the following questions:

1. Which task lasts the longest?
2. Which week is the busiest?
3. Throughout the 24-week period, which five tasks are worked on in isolation?
4. How many different tasks are worked on in week 14?
5. If all the tasks could be completed concurrently, how many weeks would the company save?
6. If all the tasks had to be completed sequentially, how many additional weeks would this add to the project?

Example answers on page 249

Flowcharts

Flowcharts are used to map the flow of progress in a system.

Flowcharts can be used to map out an overall approach to a process in vague terms, but can also be used to communicate control systems in a very detailed way; they are often used to control stock and production levels.

The flowchart below shows the steps a cashier goes through each time they serve a customer. This flowchart makes use of the five most common flowchart symbols.

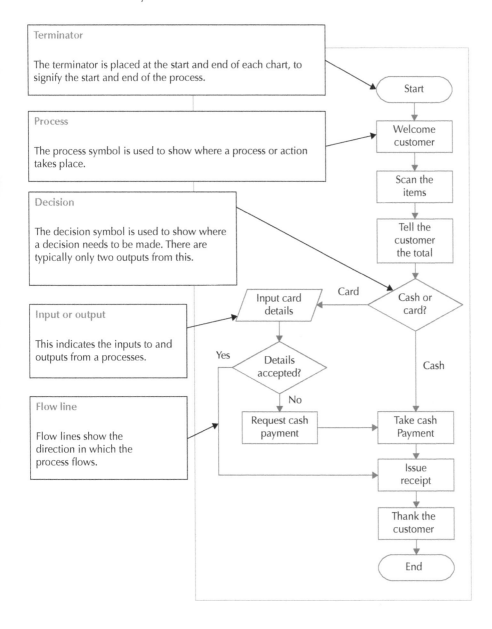

Terminator

The terminator is placed at the start and end of each chart, to signify the start and end of the process.

Process

The process symbol is used to show where a process or action takes place.

Decision

The decision symbol is used to show where a decision needs to be made. There are typically only two outputs from this.

Input or output

This indicates the inputs to and outputs from a processes.

Flow line

Flow lines show the direction in which the process flows.

Skill builder 38.2: Flowcharts

An incomplete flowchart detailing the steps required to make buttered toast is shown below.

Using the steps given and the symbols shown below, complete the flowchart for making and buttering toast.

- Wait for bread to toast
- Start
- Want it buttered?
- Need more slices?
- Place bread into toaster
- Select slice of bread
- Plug in toaster
- Set toaster timer
- Yes
- No
- Toaster plugged in?

Example answers on page 249

Scan for flowchart worksheets

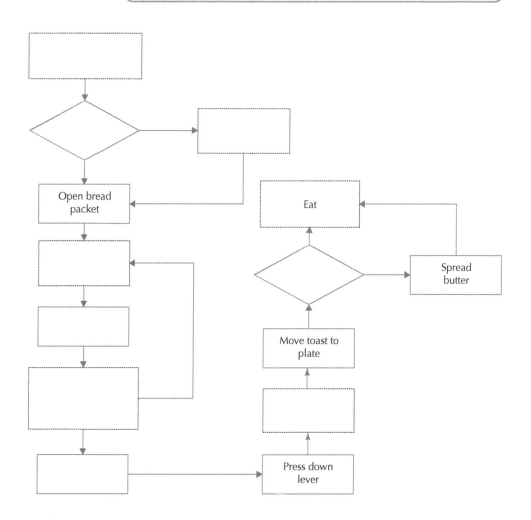

Types of production

There are many different factors that influence the type of production system that is used in the manufacture of a product. Manufacturers take great care when deciding which system to use.

Factors such as the volume of production, the complexity of the product, the most suitable manufacturing method, skill level of the available personnel and the degree of risk associated with launching the product into the marketplace need to be considered.

Three main production systems are commonly used (see below).

Mass or flow production

Companies use mass production to make large numbers of identical products, often involving line, cell or just-in-time (JIT) manufacturing setups. Mass production requires more initial investment in tooling and uses a smaller, less skilled workforce on the shop floor, due to the increased use of computer numerically control led (CNC) machines. Before companies opt for mass production, they need to be sure of the demand for the product and have the financial backing to set up the production system.

Batch production

In batch production, components or goods are produced in groups (or batches) and not in a continuous stream. Batch production systems allow for greater flexibility as the manufacturing facilities are not designed around the production of one particular product or part.

One-off or job production

When a small number of products is required, one-off production is used. This method of production is labour intensive and requires a high degree of skill on the part of the craftsperson. One-off products tend to have a much higher price tag than products that are produced in higher numbers due to the time and skill levels required to make them.

Skill builder 38.3: Which type of production setup?

Line, cell and just-in-time (JIT) manufacturing systems are commonly used within mass production environments.

Carry out research into these systems and produce a series of cue cards that list the advantages and disadvantages of each system. These cue cards can be used in preparation for the final exam.

Example answers on page 250

A range of different methods is used to make the manufacture of products faster, more accurate and, in some cases, safer.

Templates

Companies use templates to mark out the profile and position of holes and other features of a product. The use of templates speeds up production and increases accuracy.

Templates can be made in a range of different materials depending on the form of the part and the number of times the manufacturer intends to use the template. If the template is to be used in a job production or a batch production system where low numbers are to be produced, a card or paper template may be suitable, whereas a more robust metal template may be required in a mass production setup. The template of the bulkhead for a customised van (shown left) was made from MDF because of the internal cutouts.

Jigs and fixtures

Jigs and fixtures are often used in the manufacture and assembly of components.

- A jig is a device that ensures that processes such as drilling, boring and countersinking are carried out in the correct location. Jigs do this by ensuring that the component is held in the correct position, resulting in accuracy and repeatability.

- A fixture is a work holding device. It positions the work but doesn't guide, locate or position the cutting tool. Fixtures are used solely to hold the part in place to allow manufacturing or assembly operations to be carried out.

The use of jigs and fixtures makes manufacturing quicker and accurate at a reduced cost.

Standard components

Nuts, bolts, screws and washers are possibly the most common standard components used today, but the term 'standard component' covers a wide range of items that are used on a number of different products. The term is best defined as any pre-prepared item used in the production of another product. Power supplies for computers, batteries for electrical products, screens for TVs and oil filters for cars are all examples of standard components that are used on a wide range of different models.

Companies use standard components for a number of reasons.

- Standard components can be manufactured in high numbers quickly and accurately by specialists. This provides economies of scale, reducing the overall cost of producing the individual part.

- Manufacturers can focus on the development of their specialist product without having to design every individual component part.

- There is no investment needed to buy machines or train staff to manufacture parts that can be outsourced.

- Setting up production systems is made easier and is more adaptable.

The development and use of CNC machines revolutionised the manufacturing world, allowing manufacturers to produce more complex parts accurately and at much higher volumes.

Before investing in CNC machinery, the manufacturer must look at the advantages and disadvantages that CNC machining will bring.

Advantages

- CNC machines increase productivity as they can run 24 hours a day, seven days a week, with minimal interruption.
- CNC program files are highly repeatable, accurately producing the same part time and time again with minimal errors.
- Alterations to the product can be made quickly and easily by reprogramming the machine.
- Modern four-axis CNC machines can produce highly complex parts that a human operator could not.

Disadvantages

- The initial expense is great because CNC machines are more expensive than their manually operated equivalents.
- CNC machines require expensive tools.
- Productivity downtime may result when retraining the existing workforce.
- CNC machines do not completely eliminate errors. Operators are still required to run the machines, make correct alignments and to position parts on a jig.

Having considered the advantages and disadvantages, the manufacturer must also take into account their projected orders, to work out how long the machine will take to pay for itself. Manufacturers are unlikely to invest in new machinery if they do not have the projected orders to allow the machine to pay for itself within a three-year period, for example.

Skill builder 38.4: CNC

The use of CNC machines in industry is commonplace, bringing many benefits to the manufacturer.

Describe how the benefits to a manufacturer may impact on the consumer.

Example answers on page 250

CAD/CAM

To make full use of the capabilities of CNC machines, they are best integrated into a Computer Aided Design/Computer Aided Manufacture (CAD/CAM) production system.

The use of CAD/CAM allows for the creation of a pathway between the design and manufacture of the product. This greatly streamlines the system, allowing for the automated programming of CNC machines.

When choosing to integrate the design and manufacture of a product, companies benefit from all the advantages associated with the use of CNC machines but will have to weigh up the advantages and disadvantages associated with linking design and manufacture.

Advantages

- The CNC files do not have to be done on the same site as the actual manufacture.
- CAD/CAM systems are hugely efficient and often result in a reduction in the number of staff required, resulting in reduced wage bills.
- Reduction of waste and tighter controls on finances result from better monitoring of material and stock levels (JIT).
- The CAD files can be used to test the product through 3D modelling prior to any actual manufacture taking place.

Disadvantages

- The implementation of a CAM facility can be very expensive, due to the initial set-up cost and the cost associated with training staff to use any new software.

Skill builder 38.5: CAD/CAM

The use of CAD/CAM setups greatly benefits the manufacturer, but there are also negative aspects.

Describe the negative impact of the use of CAD/CAM on a traditional manufacturing workshop.

Example answers on page 250

39. Society, the environment and the wider world

Designers face many ethical dilemmas when designing products. How they respond to these impacts on society, the environment and the wider world.

Sustainability and its impact on the environment

Designing products that are sustainable greatly reduces the impact they have on our world. Sustainability goes beyond the principles of **reduce**, **reuse** and **recycle**. Truly sustainable design must consider all aspects of the product's lifecycle, from the sourcing of the raw materials, through to the product's eventual disposal.

We can expand on the commonly used 3Rs (reduce, reuse and recycle); a more thorough approach to sustainable design can be achieved when the design of the product considers 6Rs.

When designing products using the 6Rs, ask the following questions:

Rethink – is there actually a need for this new product?

Designing from this starting point will help reduce the number of products in the marketplace, reacting to consumer needs rather than wants.

Refuse – what impact does the manufacture have on the environment? Make active choices not to use particular materials unless the benefit of doing so outweighs any negative impact of the product's production and use on people and the environment.

Reduce – can the product be manufactured using less material or energy?

Reducing the amount of energy used during the production, in addition to cutting down on the amount of material used, will help reduce the product's overall impact on the environment.

Reuse – can the product, or parts of it, be used to make another product?

Designing products that can be easily used to make something else will enhance the product's value to the wider world.

Repair – can the product be designed in a way that allows for repair?

Allowing products to be repaired increases their lifespan and reduces the amount of waste.

Recycle – how easily can the product be recycled?

Designing products that can be easily recycled by consumers increases the likelihood of the materials being reprocessed.

A product that is designed using the 6Rs approach may be more expensive to produce, but it will have the least possible impact on the environment.

Skill builder 39.1: Applying the 6Rs

Select and analyse a product using the questions associated with the 6Rs, to help identify aspects of the product that could be redesigned to be more sustainable.

A low-cost, low-tech product may provide the best focus for this task, allowing for a detailed consideration of materials and construction methods.

Example answers on page 251

Balancing conflicting issues

Balancing issues such as the environment, economics, social and cultural beliefs requires careful consideration. These issues often conflict, resulting in dilemmas for the designer. Products should be designed to meet the needs of society and the wider world as well as the wants of consumers.

In particular, environmental and economic issues often conflict. Designing a product by focusing solely on the economics inevitably leads to environmental concerns, because the least expensive materials and manufacturing processes often have the greatest negative impact on the environment. For example, the use of concrete as a building material for eco-houses has many economical benefits, in terms of optimising the building and running costs of the house. However, the environmental impact of the CO_2 emitted during the production of the concrete is huge, accounting for 5% of the world's annual total.

The use of child labour in developing countries often causes consumers in the developed world to question their choices when buying products. These modern **social values** are at odds with the **cultural beliefs** of those producing the products, who often see the work as a valuable source of income that, in many cases, is essential for a family to survive. As a result of this, designers and manufacturers often commit only to use manufacturers who pledge not to use child labour or to exploit adult workers, choosing instead to opt into Fairtrade-type agreements.

As the marketplace has become more competitive, designers and producers have become more aware of the importance of considering issues surrounding the environment, economic factors, social expectations and cultural beliefs.

The outcome of balancing these issues will impact not only the economic success of the product, but also how the product is viewed by the public. If the balance is tipped too far in any direction, the risk of product failure increases greatly.

Skill builder 39.2: Balancing social and cultural issues

In recent years, Indonesian mines have been associated with the illegal mining of tin for use in the production of high-tech devices. This has caused social and cultural conflict.

Research production of other materials that may cause social and cultural conflict. Your research should include:

- details of the impact on the local population
- how the material serves the needs and wants of the end users.

You can use a mind map to explore the issues that may arise.

Example answers on page 252

Skill builder 39.3: Balancing conflicting issues

The low-cost unbranded hoodie shown was produced in the developing world before being shipped to numerous outlets across the developed world.

Using the sustainability questions from page 193 as a starting point, identify any environmental, economic, social and cultural belief conflicts associated with the manufacture and use of the hoodie.

You may use a mind map to record any conflicts, before suggesting ways in which these could be resolved.

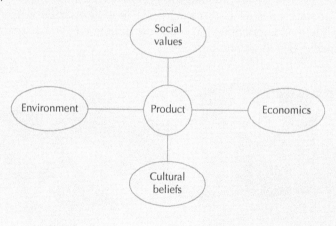

Example answers on page 253

Designing for recycling

New European environmental laws have resulted in companies having to address the issue of sustainability and designing for recycling as a priority, if they wish to remain competitive and open to new markets.

Products that are designed with recycling in mind fall into two distinct categories: recycled and recyclable products.

Recycled products

These are manufactured using recycled materials or components from products that have been used previously.

The (PET) bottles shown on the left can now be recycled into yarn and used in the manufacture of synthetic (polyester) fleece.

Recyclable products

Recyclable products, on the other hand, are manufactured to be easily recycled after use.

A modular approach is taken to the design and manufacture of the product, allowing easy dismantling for repair or reuse of the individual modules in other products. Taking this approach also influences the production methods used for the different components and the way in which different parts are joined together.

This modular approach can be seen when we look inside a computer. A computer is made up of a series of modules that can be removed and replaced during the working life of the product, or removed and reused in other products when the life of the parent product has come to an end.

Producing products in modular form often results in cost savings that can be passed on to the consumer, as each module essentially becomes a standard component that can be produced by a specialist manufacturer in high numbers.

Manufacturers are becoming more aware of the need for consumers to be able to identify what products are made of. A series of codes and symbols are used to help with this.

Recyclable products often make good use of mono-materials and use a series of codes and symbols to show what they are made from.

Identifying different materials in this way allows the end user (or recycling companies) to break the product down into smaller parts that can be recycled efficiently. This reduces the recycling cost and helps maintain the quality of the recycled material. If impurities or foreign bodies get caught within material during the recycling process, this has a direct impact on the quality of the recycled product. There is a limit to the number of times a material can be recycled because materials can become increasingly degraded the more times they are recycled.

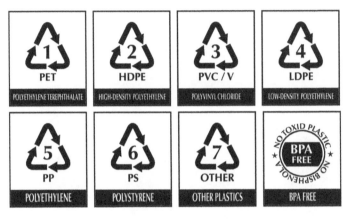

FOOD GRADE PLASTIC SYMBOL - EPS 10

Manufacturers are now also giving details of any fillers or fibres that are added to plastics to help make the component parts easier to recycle.

The photo below shows the material identification marker from the inside of a sandwich toaster. The manufacturer has identified the base material as PBT, but the additional text indicates that the material has had 20% GF (glass fibres) added.

Amt.

apper

list

SECTION 3:
Appendix

ANTHROPOMETRIC DATA FOR SKILL BUILDER 4.3

		Male			Female		
		5th	50th	95th	5th	50th	95th
Hip width	Age 5	185	208	237	191	212	249
	Age 6	187	213	246	192	218	264
	Age 8	212	242	282	218	250	306
Shoulder width	Age 5	247	271	302	252	271	304
	Age 6	253	281	317	256	281	323
	Age 8	289	319	358	283	315	368
Height	Age 5	1039	1126	1213	1044	1126	1208
	Age 6	1106	1186	1266	1089	1158	1281
	Age 8	1229	1313	1398	1202	1300	1398
Seated butt	Age 5	569	615	663	576	614	660
	Age 6	599	643	686	589	642	694
	Age 8	652	696	741	641	690	740
Back of knee height	Age 5	245	276	307	250	277	305
	Age 6	267	297	327	260	296	331
	Age 8	299	327	354	292	326	360
Adult height	British	1531	1745	1858	1510	1613	1715
	Chinese	1461	1691	1792	1501	1589	1648
	American	1643	1758	1873	1515	1621	1726

All dimensions are given in mm.

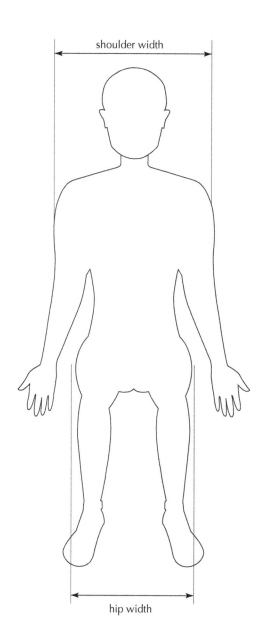

shoulder width

hip width

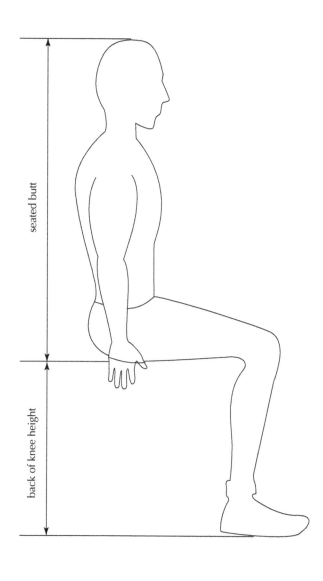

seated butt

back of knee height

SECTION 4:
Skill builder example answers

SKILL BUILDER 1.1

Roles and responsibilities of the design team members are shown below.

Designer	Provides the initial inspiration and creative input for the product and controls the product development.
Market researcher	Conducts research and provides feedback on the needs and wants of the consumers. They also provide feedback on the views of the consumer in relation to pricing, trends and projected sales numbers.
Accountant	Monitors the costs during all stages of the design process, setting caps on spending during various stages to ensure that the product can be produced and marketed at a cost the public is willing to pay.
Engineer	Tests the various aspects of the product's function, ensuring products function safely and correctly.
Manufacturer	Provides information on how a product best be manufactured and offers advice to the design team as to how a product may need to be altered to allow it to be manufactured economically and efficiently.
Lawyer	Ensures all legal aspects of a product's design, production, marketing and retail comply with the legislation of the country of sale.
Materials technologist	Provides information on all aspects of materials, from their properties to the manufacturing methods that can be used.
Production specialist	Provides information on all aspects of a product's production, from the rate and volume of production to the best production system.
Marketing team	Uses the information provided by market researchers to help publicise the product effectively and often focus on the 3Ps: price, promotion and product.
Ergonomist	Provides information on anthropometrics, physiology and psychology. They use information on gender and age range provided by market researchers to help make the data they provide specific to the intended target market.
Consumer	Provides feedback on all aspects of the product. Their feedback is vital at all stages of the product development through to the aftersales experience.
Retailer	Provides feedback on sales rates and on what is likely to sell or not.
Economist	Monitors market trends and predicts how the economy will be by the time the product reaches the marketplace. Works closely with the accountants to make sure that the product will be economically viable.
Sub-contractor	Provides expertise and services in a range of different fields. They work closely with materials technologists, production specialists, engineers and accountants to ensure the product is manufactured as efficiently as possible.

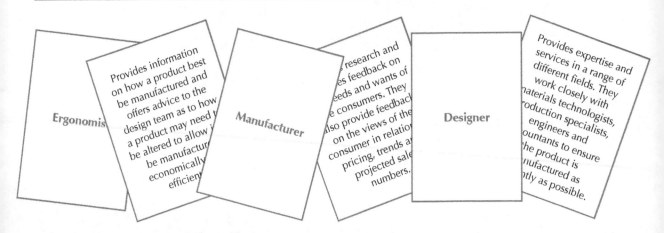

SKILL BUILDER 1.2

The different lines of communication that take place between the design team members are shown below.

Note: not all communication is two-way.

SKILL BUILDER 1.3

The implications of not balancing the inputs from each of the three types of design team members are explained below.

1

The balance of inputs from the three types of influencers is pretty good here, with a reasonable balance between the three having been struck. However, the problem is that the creative input has not been as strong as it could have, resulting in a design that has considered the technical and business aspects to the detriment of the creative aspect. The resulting product may be technically very good, designed, marketed and manufactured within budget, but be ordinary and uninspiring.

2

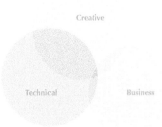

In this situation, the creative and technical types have combined well, resulting in a product that is innovative and technically very good. The business side of the partnership seems to be letting the product down, resulting in the product potentially being late to the marketplace and produced outwith the budget. This lack of input from the business thinkers could also result in the product having an inflated retail cost in a bid to claw back some of the additional costs incurred due to running over budget.

3

The creative and business thinkers have combined well in this situation, but have been let down by the technical side. The finished product is likely to be innovative and well marketed but is likely to have technical failings. The product may sell well initially, but there might be an increased number of product returns or even the need for a product recall as a result of a technical fault that came to light after the product launch.

4

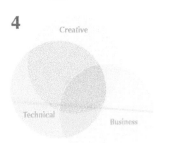

This appears to be the best balance of inputs, resulting in an innovative, technically advanced product that has been managed well throughout the design and production stages. The product is also likely to be marketed well, resulting in good sales figures and a low number of returns due to any faults. The risk here is that the product is too creative and technologically advanced, resulting in a product that is not what the market requires.

SKILL BUILDER 2.1

The J-me Squeeze-me and the Juicy Salif have both been designed for the primary function of juicing fruits such as lemons.

If the 'form follows function' rule is followed, both products will be designed to ensure they work to their optimum. The aesthetics should not detract from the functionality of the product and are likely to be thought about after the designer has ensured the greatest functionality of the product.

In the case of the Squeeze-me lemon squeezer, aesthetics have taken second place to function. The product separates, allowing the fruit to be placed inside. Parts are fitted together before the soft plastic outer is squeezed, forcing juice down the narrow funnel, ensuring no mess or loss of juice. The long funnel part also collects pips, preventing them from entering the filtered juice. The clear plastic part allows the user to see the fruit inside, adding to the ease of use and allowing the user to decide when the fruit should be changed. Form follows function had been applied with this product in several ways. An example of this is that the form of the juicer is dictated by the fruit it holds.

The Juicy Salif is different. It is very attractive and many people buy it purely as a decorative item. Function came second to aesthetics with this product. It is designed to stand out and be decorative, rather than be stored away from sight in a drawer or cupboard like the Squeeze-me. The Juicy Salif does not have a way to collect the juice or to separate the pips. The user can hold onto one of the legs to stabilise the juicer when in use. The process of juicing with this product is messy.

SKILL BUILDER 2.2

1. The purpose of the product is to produce directional light. The lamp is free standing and operates from a mains power supply. The light can be switched easily on and off. The angle of the lamp can be adjusted by hand.

2. After plugging into the mains power supply, a switch is pressed to allow power to flow through the lamp and up to the bulb where the electricity is transformed into light. The stand and lamp head can be moved and adjusted to direct the light to suit the user's needs. The light can be turned off by pressing the switch or unplugging at any time.

3. The large switch that is attached to the cable makes the product easy to turn on and off without having to use the mains plug. The heavy, round base supports the product, making it possible to readjust the top part to different angles. The collar attached to the base provides strength for the stand and helps secure the adjustable stand to the base.

4. The brackets at the pivot points keep the components of the moving stand together, making it possible to adjust the lamp whilst maintaining the form. These also provide a housing for the cable when set at any angle.

5. The shade helps to direct the light from the bulb. The large area on the back of the shade provides a housing for the bulb and provides an area to grip when adjusting the angle of the shade.

SKILL BUILDER 2.3

1. The chair is designed for indoor occasional use. The user sits centrally on the seat area, with their legs in front of them and their feet on the floor. The user would sit with their back against the backrest.

2. A variety of uses such as: stand on it, swing on it, straddle it, drag it by the back, hang clothes on it, use it outdoors.

3. If sat on and used as intended, the product would be able to hold the user's weight and would be stable. If stood on, there may be too much weight and the leg joints may give way. If swung on, the product may fall over backwards or the back legs may weaken or snap off. If straddled, the product will still function. If dragged, the legs may become scuffed or damaged. If clothes are hung on it, the backrest may experience more wear. If too many clothes are placed on the back, the product may topple. If used outdoors, the product will still function although the materials may weaken or rot if not protected from the weather.

4. Redesign the chair with additional functions. There are other possible answers to this task.

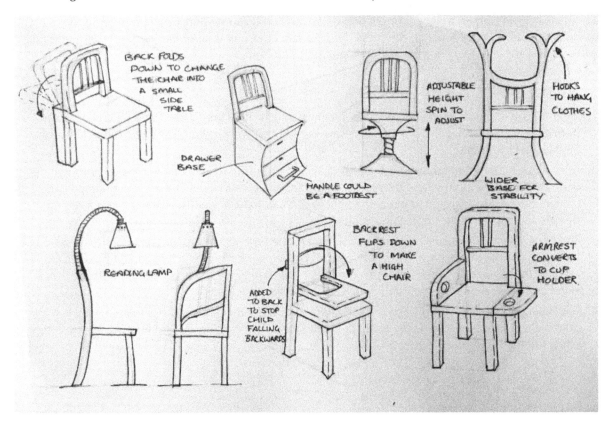

SKILL BUILDER 3.1

Visual, colour – Both rooms use a mixture of the same warm and cool colours. The cream colour of the walls and the furniture adds warmth to the hospital room. This is more comforting than a sterile white room. The blue bed cover stands out, making this the dominant feature in the room. In the second room the blue colour is used in the rug to create a sense of space and in the pillows to add decoration. A crisp white is used, creating a fresh feel.

Visual, shape and line – There are a lot of contrasting shapes and lines used in the hospital room, including the furniture and walls. This makes the room very busy and potentially unsettling for the patient. The bedroom uses mainly squares, creating an orderly look. The contrasting curve of the headboard and curved edges of the bedside furniture creates a more relaxed feel.

Visual, symmetry – In the bedroom symmetry reinforces the neat orderly look. There is no symmetry in the hospital room; it is packed with equipment.

Sound – There is potentially a lot of noise from the items in the hospital room. Noise could come from other patients behind the screen, as well as from the machines. This could be unsettling for the patient. The bedroom is more likely to be a quiet and intimate space.

Smell – All hospitals have a smell, from the chemicals, cleaning materials and furniture. The bedroom would be more relaxing for the user as it would smell familiar.

Tactile, texture – Many of the surfaces in the hospital room are smooth, making them hygienic and easy to wipe clean. The bedroom textures are softer and more comfortable.

SKILL BUILDER 3.2

The shape of the 500 has evolved over time. It has gradually become more curvy as the transition between the bonnet and the roof is now a more subtle angle.

The modern Fiat 500 is larger than the early models, although the traditional bold yellow colour is still available.

Use of line is evident in both cars. There is alignment between the bottom of the windows and the height of the bonnet. In the new model, a contrasting black has been used in the edges of the windows to create an illusion of more defined, sharper shaped windows.

Pattern has been used to add interest and perceived value to the wheels. The introduction of alloys has made the more intricate pattern possible on the modern fiat.

The bumpers in the older car are metal, standing out from the car, whereas the new car's bumpers are built into the body and are the same colour, making for a clean simple design.

The proportion of the wheels to the car has changed over time. Wheels have become bigger. This may attract more buyers as it gives the car a better overall look.

Metal on the older car is dull, whereas a high polished chrome is used in the new Fiat. This creates a higher perceived value.

New-car smell is appealing to some consumers. The used smell of a vintage car may not appeal to some, particularly if the previous owner smoked.

Engine noise also influences users. Some might want a quiet drive whilst others prefer to hear the sound of their engine. The old car may produce noises that could affect the driver's confidence in the reliability or safety of the car.

The older car may be appealing today as people like to have vintage products, either as nostalgic things or because they like the aesthetic appeal of vintage products. The new car may be appealing because of its colour and size.

SKILL BUILDER 3.3

Aesthetic elements

The decisions about the aesthetics of a product have a direct impact on other aspects, such as function, ergonomics, material and manufacturing.

The **colour** of the iron is cooling. Different shades of the colour blue are used to identify functions and components of the iron. The buttons are the deepest colour. The heat control dial is pale to contrast with the body, so users can see it. The cord is the same colour as the handle. This makes it look like a natural extension of the product. The areas for pouring in and storing the water are transparent, to allow the user to check the water level.

The white **colour** at the base is clean-looking, which users may associate with their clean laundry.

The front **shape/form** is pointed, getting wider towards the back. This improves the function as it will push creases to the side.

Curved **lines** are used on the handle. These give the impression the handle is comfortable to hold. This, together with the form, suggests the motion of moving forward.

Symmetry is evident. The buttons are positioned to be symmetrical, as is the pattern on the base.

The **pattern** on the base complements the shape. The pattern indicates where the steam comes out.

The iron is in good **proportion**. The steam and water jet buttons are large to make them easy to press. The heat dial is slim, so as not to interfere with the hand clearance area.

The harmonising colours, stable shape and symmetry all help with the visual **balance** of the product.

Transparent plastic **material** has been used to indicate the water sections. The main white body has a smooth texture, making it easy to clean and maintaining the aesthetics. The pale-coloured handle is made from a rubbery material. This **texture** provides improved comfort and grip during use, but is likely to retain dirt, which in time will make the iron look tatty. The plate at the bottom is a sliver-coloured teflon-coated metal, which heats up and glides easily.

There is minimum **smell** from the iron. A slight smell from the plastic materials is evident, but this would not negatively impact the user experience.

There are several **sounds** that help indicate the operation and use of the iron. As the iron reaches temperature, there is a sound created by steam release to alert the user. As the temperature is adjusted, the dial clicks. Sound is also present when the water and steam buttons are pressed.

The iron is a reasonable **weight** to use. It feels good **quality**, gives the impression it will iron out creases and isn't too heavy, thus avoiding fatigue.

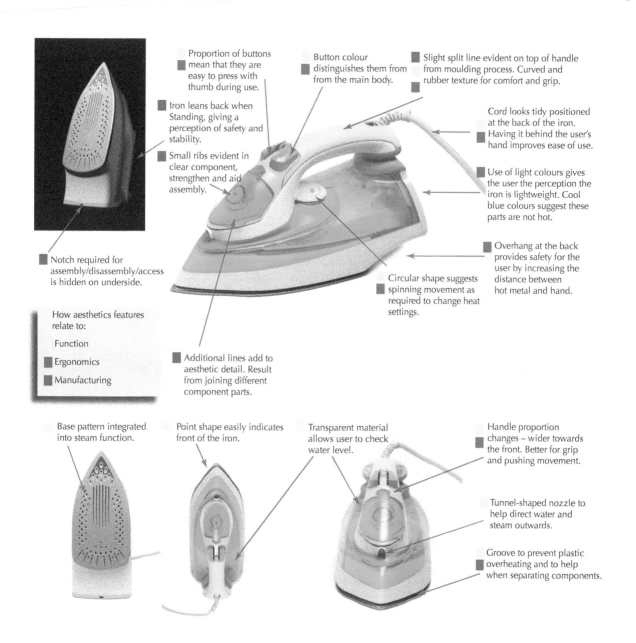

Proportion of buttons mean that they are easy to press with thumb during use.

Button colour distinguishes them from from the main body.

Slight split line evident on top of handle from moulding process. Curved and rubber texture for comfort and grip.

Iron leans back when Standing, giving a perception of safety and stability.

Cord looks tidy positioned at the back of the iron. Having it behind the user's hand improves ease of use.

Small ribs evident in clear component, strengthen and aid assembly.

Use of light colours gives the user the perception the iron is lightweight. Cool blue colours suggest these parts are not hot.

Notch required for assembly/disassembly/access is hidden on underside.

Overhang at the back provides safety for the user by increasing the distance between hot metal and hand.

Circular shape suggests spinning movement as required to change heat settings.

How aesthetics features relate to:

Function

Ergonomics

Manufacturing

Additional lines add to aesthetic detail. Result from joining different component parts.

Base pattern integrated into steam function.

Point shape easily indicates front of the iron.

Transparent material allows user to check water level.

Handle proportion changes – wider towards the front. Better for grip and pushing movement.

Tunnel-shaped nozzle to help direct water and steam outwards.

Groove to prevent plastic overheating and to help when separating components.

SKILL BUILDER 3.4

Remember to annotate

- Improve the function by making the toast easier to remove

- Make it easy to clean

- Make it easier to manufacture

- Increase the stability of the product

- Make it safer to use

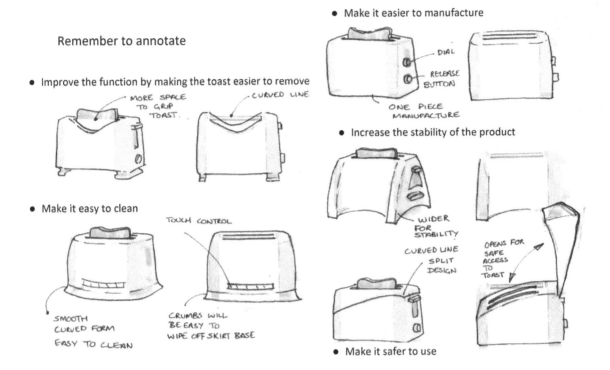

SKILL BUILDER 3.5

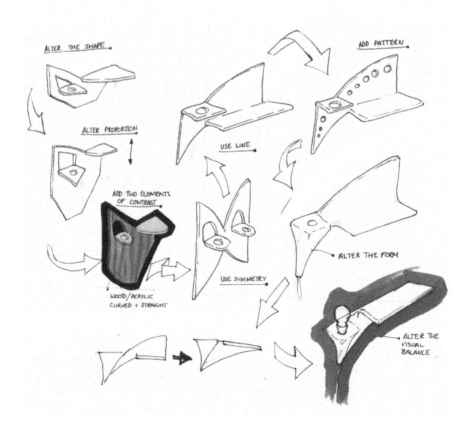

SKILL BUILDER 4.1

The chair needs to be comfortable for the user, so the width and length of the chair need to accommodate a range of users.

It needs to adjust to the correct height for the dentist. The chair must adjust in height and angle to allow the dentist to see and work in the patient's mouth.

The tools must be easy to access and store. There must be enough clearance space between the tools to allow a large adult male hand to grip and remove each tool. There also needs to be some clearance space in the tool slots, so that no force is required to remove or store the tools.

The pedal needs to be easy to press and the foot pedal needs to be within easy reach of the dentist's foot. The surface area (width and length) of the pedal should be easy to press by all users, accommodating different foot sizes. The pedal should operate with reasonable force and effort, so it can be pressed from a seated position.

The chair should not distress the patients. The noise of the chair and tools should not be alarming. This is also important so that the dentist is not distracted. The colours should be cool and calming to relax the patient.

Any bad smells might make the patient question the hygiene of the dental surgery. The chair should be made from an easy-clean fabric, so as not to hold smells or stains.

The mirror needs to be easy to use. It must be within comfortable reach of the dentist and require reasonable force and effort to pull and push it into position.

The dental tools should be easy and safe to use. They need to be long enough to allow the dentist to grip them, as well as to access the patient's mouth. The tools should not be too heavy as this would cause the dentist's muscles to fatigue, which may result in injury to the patient. If the tools are too light, the dentist might perceive them as poor quality.

SKILL BUILDER 4.2

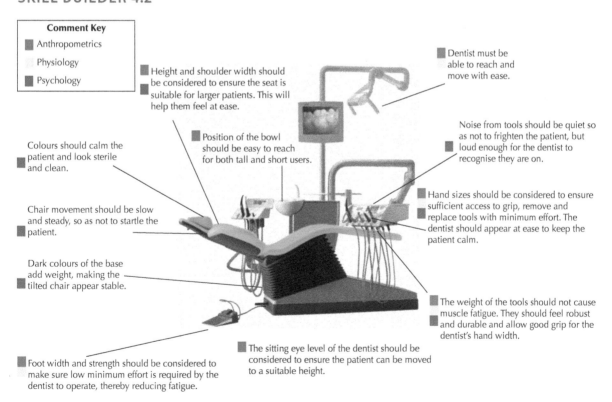

Comment Key
■ Anthropometrics
□ Physiology
■ Psychology

■ Height and shoulder width should be considered to ensure the seat is suitable for larger patients. This will help them feel at ease.

■ Dentist must be able to reach and move with ease.

■ Colours should calm the patient and look sterile and clean.

■ Position of the bowl should be easy to reach for both tall and short users.

■ Noise from tools should be quiet so as not to frighten the patient, but loud enough for the dentist to recognise they are on.

■ Chair movement should be slow and steady, so as not to startle the patient.

■ Hand sizes should be considered to ensure sufficient access to grip, remove and replace tools with minimum effort. The dentist should appear at ease to keep the patient calm.

■ Dark colours of the base add weight, making the tilted chair appear stable.

■ The weight of the tools should not cause muscle fatigue. They should feel robust and durable and allow good grip for the dentist's hand width.

■ Foot width and strength should be considered to make sure low minimum effort is required by the dentist to operate, thereby reducing fatigue.

■ The sitting eye level of the dentist should be considered to ensure the patient can be moved to a suitable height.

SKILL BUILDER 4.3

Part of playground	Minimum size (mm)	Size from table
Diameter of flume slide – to fit all children sliding	368	Age 8 girl 95$^{th\%ile}$ shoulder width
Width of red slide – up to age 5	249	Age 5 boy 95$^{th\%ile}$
Height of red roof – up to age 6 children standing	1281	Age 6 girl 95$^{th\%ile}$ height
Height of opening to flume slide – all children sitting	741	Age 8 boy 95$^{th\%ile}$ seated butt to head
Height of swing frame to allow all adults clearance	1873	American adult male 95$^{th\%ile}$ height
Height of swing seat – allow all children to sit safely	245	Age 5 boy 5$^{th\%ile}$ back of knee height

SKILL BUILDER 4.4

Activity	With/without glove	Time taken	Ease of use	Key difficulties
Pick up a pencil and write the alphabet	without	16s	Very	None
	with	29s	Some difficulty	Picking up and gripping the pencil
Use a key to unlock a door	without	5s	Minor difficulty	Lining up the key with the lock
	with	33s	Difficult	Gripping the correct part of the key with enough force to turn
Open a drinks bottle	without	3s	Very	None
	with	Not complete	Too difficult	Unable to close fingers to grip the bottle lid

I decided to model a solution to help people use a key to lock and unlock a door.

This cone shape model didn't work too well. It was still difficult to locate the key and the lock. The lock was also no longer visible.

I reversed the cone shape. This made it easier to see the lock and it helped guide the key towards the lock.

Flattening and shortening the top area improved the aesthetics and visibility of the lock, making it easier to use. This design helped guide the key to the lock, although the opening was a bit too wide.

The final design could be die cast as part of the door handle itself as shown opposite. The user can bring the key down from the top, then the sloped walls help guide the key towards the lock.

SKILL BUILDER 4.5

	Step		Sending a text
1	Forming a goal	**What do I want?**	To send a text message
2	Forming the intention	**What would satisfy this goal?**	Using a mobile phone
3	Specifying an action	**What do I have to do to achieve the intention?**	Unlock the phone, use the message app, select a contact, type in the message and press send
4	Executing the action	**Do the steps I have specified.**	Unlocked, selected message app and contact, typed message and pressed send
5	Perceiving the state of the world	**Use my senses to gather information about the world and/or system I am working in.**	Woosh sound when pressing send. No vibration feedback?
6	Interpreting the state of the world	**Figure out what, if anything, has changed.**	Has the message sent? Text tells me it is delivered
7	Evaluating the outcome	**Did I achieve my goal?**	Yes

	Step		Making toast
1	Forming a goal	**What do I want?**	To toast bread
2	Forming the intention	**What would satisfy this goal?**	Using a grill or toaster
3	Specifying an action	**What do I have to do to achieve the intention?**	Put the bread in the slot, set to medium, press lever to pull toast down and switch on
4	Executing the action	**Do the steps I have specified.**	Completed steps above
5	Perceiving the state of the world	**Use my senses to gather information about the world and/or system I am working in.**	Some noise from toaster when it is on, when pushed down lever clicks and stays down when on, can smell the bread as it toasts
6	Interpreting the state of the world	**Figure out what, if anything, has changed.**	Bread has toasted and turned brown and crispy, lever has popped up bringing toast up with it
7	Evaluating the outcome	**Did I achieve my goal?**	Yes

SKILL BUILDER 4.6

1. **The lift: Sight** – This could enhance the user's experience of the lift as they view the surroundings and enjoy the journey. It could also have a negative impact and instil fear in those with vertigo. **Sound** – If smooth and consistent, this will calm the user during use. Other sounds can alert the user when the doors are opening or closing or when they have arrived at a floor. Squeaks and creaks will have a negative impact on the user experience and may provoke fear or uncertainty in the safety of the lift. **Smell** – being in a confined space, a fresh smell is important to the user's experience. Mechanical smell, e.g. oil may have a negative effect as they remind the user of the workings of the lift. **Feel** – The lift should move smoothly, without sudden jolts or jerks which may panic the user. The glass should feel as if it is securely held in place.

   The iron: Sight – the colour of the buttons and marks on the dials make them easier to see. A light indicates when a temperature is reached, putting the user at ease and feeling in control. The colour of the metal plate stands out, so it will not be touched by accident. **Sound** – The iron makes a little noise that helps remind the user it is on. This is an important safety feature. Noise is also present when steam is released. **Smell** – If the iron smelled bad, the user would not want to use it on their clothes, in case it burned or transferred. **Feel** – The iron needs to have a good grip, so the user feels it is safe to pick up. The base should be smooth to glide over clothes with ease – if it didn't, users may fear it would damage their garments. The user should not feel any heat whilst operating the iron because this would impact how safe they feel.

2. **The lift:** The visibility in the lift may appeal to users who want a view over the city or may deter those with fear of heights or open spaces. The glass and metal material combined with the cylindrical form gives the lift a futuristic capsule look, which may appeal to some users.

   The iron: Consumers may or may not purchase this iron due to the pink colour depending on whether they like it and on whether it matches other products or surroundings in their home. The clear mid section provides good visibility of water levels, which users may like. The form is leaning forward and tapered to look light and quick, which some users may find appealing. The steam and water buttons stand out and are a darker colour, which would prevent them showing dirt accumulated through use.

3. **The lift: Proximity** – As the distance from the ground increases, enjoyment or anxiety will also increase. If the lift is closer to the building, the users will feel more secure. **Familiarity** – If the buttons, controls, access and exit are all familiar, users will be more likely to use the lift without confusion. This would also reduce anxiety in those uncomfortable with an open lift.

   The iron: Proximity – The buttons should be within reach, allowing the user to push them without releasing their grip on the handle. If the handle is too close to the main body, it would be difficult to hold and access the dial. **Familiarity** – As the iron gets hot it is important that the user can adjust it quickly and safely. The iron can stand on its end, like most irons, and uses the standard push buttons and dials to operate and adjust settings.

SKILL BUILDER 5.1

Sports stars are often used to endorse products

Michael Jordan's partnership with **Nike** is the most successful celebrity partnership ever. In 1982, Jordan signed a five-year contract worth $2.5 million plus royalties with Nike. Jordan first wore a pair of red and black Air Jordans in his rookie year (1984) and they were banned by the league as they did not feature any white. He was fined $5000 every time he wore them on court. This created huge publicity and the Nike/Jordan partnership is still strong today. In 2013 Nike made $2.25 billion in basketball sales and it was reported that Jordan made $90 million, a decade after he last appeared on a basketball court!

The celebrity should appeal to the product's target market

From the cleanest player in football to the nation's favourite commentator, **Gary Lineker** has been the perfect face for the **Walkers** crisp brand for 19 years – making it one of the longest-running celebrity endorsements in the country.

Researchers at the Psychology Department of the University of Warwick say Lineker's value as a figurehead lies in the fact that we admire him, but we also have a sneaking suspicion that he's just like us.

A celebrity can endorse several brands

Rita Ora has endorsement deals with **Superga** shoes, **Rimmel**, **DKNY**, **Madonna's Material Girl** clothing line, **Marks & Spencer**, **Adidas Originals** and **Roberto Cavalli**.

Does celebrity endorsement work?

'Remarkably, given how much money is spent based on celebrity endorsements (celebrities appear in roughly one-fifth of ads, according to market researchers, and a single company like Nike might spend around half a billion dollars a year on endorsements), there's been very little academic research on the effect of these ads on sales.' – marketwatch.com

Sometimes endorsements backfire

Nike worked with **Lance Armstrong** for over a decade. Nike dropped its personal sponsorship of Armstrong after the U.S. Anti-Doping Agency exposed the team doping programme

George Clooney and **Nespresso** are such a good fit because both have an air of sophistication and suavity which neatly complements the other.

SKILL BUILDER 5.2

BUILDING A BRAND IDENTITY

One of the ways PUMA has built up its brand identity is through sponsorship.

PUMA sponsors a wide range of sports, as listed here.

- American football
- Australian football
- Basketball
- Boxing
- Cricket
- Fencing
- Football
- Gaelic football
- Golf
- Motor sports
- Rugby league
- Rugby union
- Sailing
- Tennis
- Track and field

PUMA sponsors a lot of sports federations, competitions, current and past players.

It sponsors players of different nationalities and ages.

Puma has also partnered with pop stars such as Rihanna, who oversees the company's womenswear line, including shoes and clothing. She was the face of the brand's autumn 2015 ad campaign.

TOUCH POINTS

Website (with newsletter sign up)

Competitions

Branded packaging

Advertising

SKILL BUILDER 5.3

Cyanide in Tylenol

In 1982 in the USA someone inserted cyanide into boxes of Tyenol (pain relief capsules) and placed them on a chemist's shelf in the Chicago area. Seven people died.

Although the manufacturers, Johnson & Johnson, weren't to blame they recalled **31 million** packets of pain relievers, which retailed at over **$100 million**.

The company survived the recall, helped by the introduction of tamper-resistant packaging.

Faulty Firestone Tyres on Ford SUVs

In 2000, Ford recalled **20 million** tyres that were fitted to their SUVs. The tyres had a disproportionate amount of tread separation and were dangerous: 174 people died and it was estimated that one out of every 4149 tyres was faulty. Ford ended up losing around **$3 billion**.

Thomas and Friends Wooden Toys

In 2007 **1.5 million units**, costing about **$60 million** were recalled because the paint used on them contained lead, which can be toxic if ingested.

Infantino Baby Sling

Some **1 million** Infantino Slingrider and Wendy Bellissimo baby slings were recalled in 2010, after they were linked to three infant deaths. The slings, which hold the child close to the mother's chest, could suffocate a baby within minutes if the fabric pressed against its nose or mouth. The cost of this recall is **irrelevant** compared to the loss of life of infants.

For further information on product recalls visit:

http://www.therichest.com/business/the-10-worst-product-recalls/

http://www.cpsc.gov/en/Recalls

SKILL BUILDER 6.1

During the lifetime of a bike, the following maintenance tasks are likely to be carried out.

- The tyres would be replaced as they wear. The frequency of this depends on how often, and for what purpose, the bike is used. This has been made easier for the user with the introduction of quick release wheels. The user does not need any tools to remove the wheel from the bike. Inexpensive equipment, such as tyre levers, are supplied to make removing the tyre easier.

- Mechanisms on the bike require regular lubrication. These parts are normally easily accessible and don't require anything to be moved or any tools to access them. Lubricant spray or oil can easily be applied to them.

- Any cables on the bike will likely need changed after a while as they will stretch. The user normally only has to adjust just one locking nut for both the gears and the brakes. This makes removing and replacing them very easy. Some adjustments might be required afterwards but these can be done with common spanner sizes.

- The seat and handlebars may require adjusting so the bike can be transported in a car. Again, only one bolt need be loosened for the seat. Normally the same sized bolt is used for the handlebar clamp. This reduces the need for lots of different tools to be used.

- Most new bikes come with a multi spanner. The designer has ensured that a common range of nut sizes are used on the bike and can be found on the spanner. This makes maintenance easier.

SKILL BUILDER 6.2

Toothbrushes, trainers, reading glasses, mobile phones and watches are all repeat purchases.

Trainers and mobile phone purchases have likely risen as a result of planned obsolescence.

New trainers are mostly purchased due to wear. However, several pairs have been replaced because they are no longer fashionable even though they could still be worn. This could be an example of planned obsolescence.

Mobile phones are often replaced as newer models become available. Although the existing phone is still usable it needs to be replaced to keep up to date with the latest operating systems, apps and other technologies.

SKILL BUILDER 6.3

Throwaway society is the name given to the linear cradle-to-grave approach to purchasing, using and disposing of products. The throwaway part refers to the throwing away of products once they have reached the end of their lifespan or are no longer of use to the consumer. Often, society throws away products even when they are still working and useful. Common examples of this are foodstuffs and mobile phones.

Consumerism is an ideology that encourages the purchasing of goods and services. It often means the purchase of goods and services that we don't particularly have need of. An example of this would be purchasing four controllers for an Xbox One when you will only ever use one or two controllers.

SKILL BUILDER 7.1

1. The designer will have considered the safety of young children. Child safety locks are present in a lot of cars. This safety feature prevents young children opening the door when the car is stationary or moving.

2. Bright lights at night can dazzle the driver and may potentially cause accidents. Dimming rear view mirrors have been designed to reduce the glare from car headlights.

3. Good visibility is essential for the driver to drive safely. Rubber windscreen wipers have been designed to clear rain and dirt off the windscreen, maintaining good visibility in poor weather.

4. Winter driving is difficult as cars can slide on the road. Many cars have digital displays that warn the driver of icy conditions.

5. Petrol and diesel are flammable substances. Modern car fuel tanks can be opened with a key or with a lever from inside the car to release the covering hatch. This prevents unwanted access to the fuel.

6. All cars are designed to have a horn. This is a safety feature that allows drivers to alert pedestrians or other drivers to their presence.

7. Cars are designed with a crumple zone. This is the area of the car that absorbs the impact of a head-on crash. This feature aims to protect the front passengers from the impact.

8. Car windows are made from special glass that doesn't shatter into sharp pieces when broken. This safety feature reduces the risk and severity of injury from broken glass in the event of a crash.

9. The driver's reaction time is important. The pedals, gears and dashboard instruments are all placed so the driver can reach them quickly and easily without taking their eyes off the road.

10. All cars are designed with a hazard light. This feature can prevent other accidents. If a car has broken down, the flashing hazards attract help but also alert other motorists to the fact that the car is stationary, avoiding any collisions.

SKILL BUILDER 7.2

Product: Road Bike			
STAGE	RISK	HAZARD	SOLUTION
RESEARCH	Medium	Not being seen at night	Use reflective paint and lights to ensure visibility
DEVELOPMENT	High	Braking distance in wet weather	Identify best brake and tyre combination through testing
MANUFACTURE	Medium – High	Injury from machines, projectiles, fumes, etc.	Train staff, keep the work space tidy and safe, maintain machines
DISTRIBUTION	Low – Medium	Weight to lift and transport	Package in more than one box Warning on box
USE	Medium	User could attempt to use off road	Marketing strategy Include instructions for use
DISPOSAL	Low	Could create unnecessary pollution	Ensure materials and components can be separated for recycling or reuse

SKILL BUILDER 8.1

SELFIE STICK	
FACTOR	REASON FOR EVALUATION
	I want to know:
Function	• Can it hold phones securely? • Can it hold a range of phones? • Does it extend far enough to work well? • Is it easy to extend? • Is it bluetooth?
Cost	• How does its price compare to similar products?
Ergonomics	• Is it light enough to manoeuvre easily/hold steady? • Does it feel well balanced? • Can it be used by a range of people?

HEDGE TRIMMER	
FACTOR	REASON FOR EVALUATION
	I want to know:
Function	• How well it cuts the hedge • How far it can reach (length of blade)
Cost	• How does it compare in price to similar products? • What are the running/maintenance costs?
Ergonomics	• Is it a reasonable weight for the target market to use? • Are all key parts (handle, switch, etc.) a suitable size for the target market?
Safety	• Does it meet required safety standards? • Does it 'feel' safe to use?
Ease of maintenance	• How often will it need to be maintained? • What maintenance is required?

TRAMPOLINE	
FACTOR	REASON FOR EVALUATION
	I want to know:
Function	• How many people can use it at one time? • What weight can it take? • How easy is it to assemble? • Are there any additional features?
Cost	• How does it compare in price to similar products?
Safety	• Does it meet appropriate safety standards? • Is it safe in use?
Durability	• Will it withstand prolonged use by the target market? • Will it withstand outdoor use without additional protection? • What maintenance is required? • Can spare parts be purchased?

TOY TRUCK	
FACTOR	REASON FOR EVALUATION
	I want to know:
Aesthetics	• Does it appeal to the target market?
Safety	• Does it meet appropriate safety standards? • Is it safe in use?
Durability	• Will it withstand use by the target market?
Ergonomics	• Can the target market play with it with ease?
Function	• Does it 'engage' the target market?

SKILL BUILDER 9.1

Test rigs are used to test a range of features on mobile phones

Repeated opening/shutting of the case

Repeated pressing of buttons

Repeated drop tests on screen

Repeated flex tests on screen

Rattle test in dust box

Repeated opening/closing of the shutter

Repeated SIM card removal

Rain, heat and moisture simulator

Repeated flex test of the casing

Drop test

SKILL BUILDER 9.2

Evaluation of Philips AT700 Aquatouch

COMPARISON TO OTHER PRODUCTS

	Philips AT799 Aquatouch	Simple Value PS-8217W	Philips S7530/50 Series 7000	Braun 799 Series 7	Remington R95 DualTrack Travel
COST	£49.99	£11.99	£300	£170	£9.99
BATTERY TIME	45 Mins	45 Mins	50 Mins	50 Mins	30 Mins
CHARGE TIME	8 Hrs	8 Hrs	8 Hrs	8 Hrs	8 Hrs
QUICK CHARGE	Yes	No	Yes	Yes	No
TRIMMER	Yes	No	Yes	Yes	No
WET & DRY	Yes	No	Yes	Yes	No
TYPE OF HEAD	GentleCut heads and Aquatec Wet and Dry. Effortlessly glides over skin using Rotary Comfort System.	Rotary system	Muliple Axis Pivoting Shaving Head. Floating cutting elements.	A unique combination of a pivoting shaver head and floating foils ensure maximum adaptability.	2 Rotary Two rotary heads

USER TRIP

I decided to try the razor and record my findings at each stage:

- **Initial impressions** – The razor fitted my hand well. It was fairly easy to figure out how to operate the razor even although the 'on' button was not very clearly marked – I pressed it intuitively.

  Getting the trimmer to flick open was a bit more tricky as I kept pushing the slide button instead of pulling it.

- **Use** – I tried the razor twice. The first time was without water and the razor gave a smooth shave. The second time I used the razor I used it with soapy water. It seemed to be smoother when I was using it but the finished result was not any smoother than the dry shave. The trimmer worked well. The only negative with the use of the razor was that it is quite noisy, particularly the trimmer.

- **Other points** – Opening the razor to clean the heads was straightforward and the actual cleaning was easy with the brushes supplied. The battery charger was easy to plug in and the razor was fully charged in eight hours, as described.

SKILL BUILDER 10.1

The list of things you can do with a brick is almost endless – here are a few ideas.

- dumbbell
- hold cars up when changing wheel
- paperweight
- stand on it to reach a high shelf
- stool
- split it and use as goalposts
- to replace table leg
- crush it and use dust in egg timer
- use as target
- swap it for two half bricks
- crack walnuts
- stop car rolling down hill
- weapon
- piece of modern art
- door stop
- plant seeds in soil in holes
- marker to race towards
- put in a cistern to save water

Here are a few of the benefits of making a car out of jelly.

- cheaper
- less likely to cause damage
- smell nice
- could be dissolved and a new one made
- eat if you're hungry
- big range of colours
- easy to park
- comfortable
- easy to customise body parts
- easy to replace
- less fatalities
- could have moulds for 'add on' bits
- less use of materials
- tyres wouldn't burst

SKILL BUILDER 10.2

TECHNOLOGY TRANSFER

SPACE JUNK COLLECTOR

The space junk collector, invented by researchers from Aalborg University, Esbjerg, is based on a basic principle used in pop-up tents and in the screens photographers use.

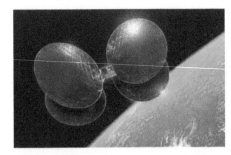

MEMORY FOAM

Temper foam was invented in 1966 by NASA for use in aeroplane seats. The foam, which flows to match the contour of whatever is pressing against it, is now used for a wide range of products, such as padding for motorcycle helmets, pillows, insoles and custom-moulded seats for use by disabled people.

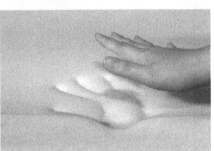

THE DUSTBUSTER

The Dustbuster cordless handheld vacuum, is used to clean up dust and crumbs around the house and was developed by Black & Decker from the same technology that helped Apollo astronauts drill for rock samples on the surface of the moon.

DIGITAL CAMERAS

In the 1990s, a team of researchers led by Eric Fossum carried out studies to significantly miniaturise cameras on board spacecraft while maintaining high image quality for scientific purposes. By June 2000, Photobit, a company Fossum helped to found had sold 1 million sensors for use in everything from digital cameras to dental radiography.

PLANT MOISTURE TEXTS

Technology developed by NASA that monitors water levels in plant leaves is now being used to send farmers text messages when their plants need to be watered.

SKILL BUILDER 10.3

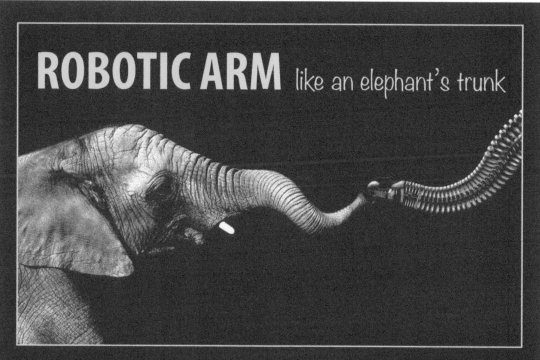

ROBOTIC ARM *like an elephant's trunk*

Inspired by the motion of an elephant's trunk, Festo AG developed the Bionic Handling Assistant, a mechantronic arm that can work closely and safely with humans. Unlike industrial robotic arms, which are typically enclosed in safety cages to protect nearby workers, the Bionic Handling Assistant is designed to interact directly with a human. Incidental contact with the mechatronic arm is harmless because the arm is made of lightweight polymer components and is driven by compressed air. Also, the pneumatics are managed by a control syastem that yields immediately in the event of a collision.

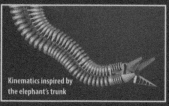

Kinematics inspired by the elephant's trunk

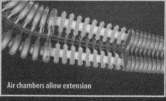

Air chambers allow extension

Hand axis positions the gripper

Movement of gripping fingers

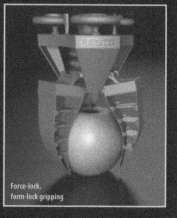

Force-lock, form-lock gripping

BIOMIMICRY *inspired by nature*

SKILL BUILDER 10.4

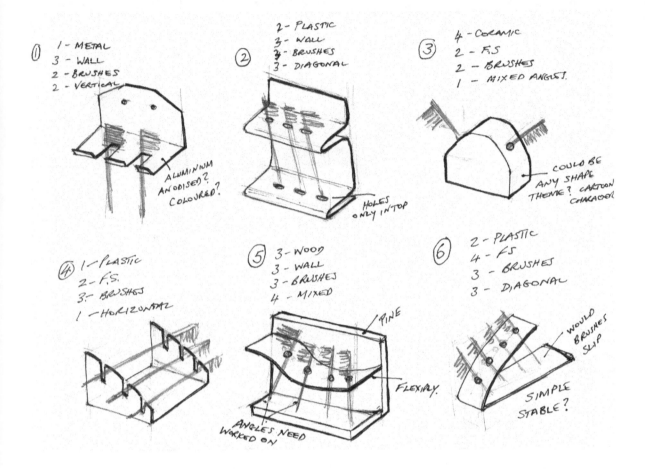

① 1 – METAL
3 – WALL
2 – BRUSHES
2 – VERTICAL

ALUMINIUM
ANODISED?
COLOURED?

② 2 – PLASTIC
3 – WALL
3 – BRUSHES
3 – DIAGONAL

HOLES
ONLY IN TOP

③ 4 – CERAMIC
2 – F.S
2 – BRUSHES
1 – MIXED ANGLES.

COULD BE
ANY SHAPE
THEME? CARTOON
CHARACTER

④ 1 – PLASTIC
2 – F.S.
3 – BRUSHES
1 – HORIZONTAL

⑤ 3 – WOOD
3 – WALL
3 – BRUSHES
4 – MIXED

PINE

FLEXIBLY.

ANGLES NEED
WORKED ON

⑥ 2 – PLASTIC
4 – F.S
3 – BRUSHES
3 – DIAGONAL

WOULD
BRUSHES
SLIP

SIMPLE
STABLE?

SKILL BUILDER 11.1

Developments that would make the alarm clock more appealing to a teenage market:

- Include a dock for music player.
- Include touchscreen technology.
- Allow it to link to other devices (game consoles, phones etc.).
- Try different colour combinations.
- Add a theme that appeals to teenagers to the design (sport team, pop artist).
- Try less symmetrical forms.
- Change the positions of the buttons to makes them easier to access and press.

SKILL BUILDER 11.2

The designer has explored:

- Different methods of mounting the holder to the wall.
- Alternative shapes for the backing plate.
- Positions of the holder on the backing plate.

SKILL BUILDER 11.3

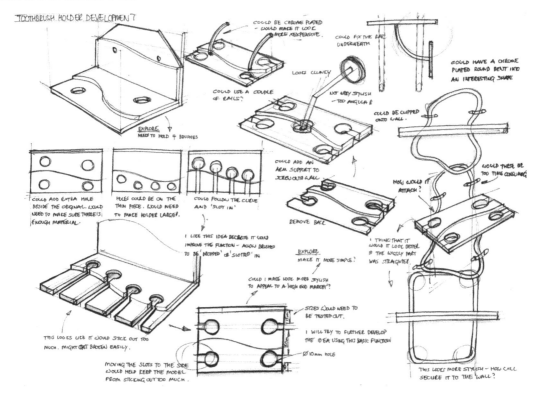

SKILL BUILDER 11.4

The designer has refined:

- The function of the holder. The way it is going to securely store the toothbrush has been decided, tested and evaluated.
- How the holder will be mounted to the wall. The designer has decided to use screws that will pass through the holder then sit in a smaller hole that will secure the screw head in place.
- The materials to be used.

SKILL BUILDER 12.1

The following annotations are useful.

- 'Material must be moulded but have electrical insulating properties'. This provides a reminder about material properties that can be referred back to later on. It also demonstrates knowledge and understanding of the properties of materials relevant to the particular type of design.

- 'Speaker cone', although very basic and simple, makes it very clear what this part of the design is. This means that the graphic does not need clarification or to be redrawn to better communicate what this part is.

- 'Filleted corners would [help] make it suitable for injection moulding'. This annotation clearly displays a good understanding of injection moulding and how plastic behaves when being injected into a mould.

The following annotations are not useful.

- 'Curvy' simply describes something that is clearly obvious from the sketch.

- 'Quite a big gap' simply describes something that is obvious from the sketch. This could be qualified by suggesting why this could be a good or bad feature.

- 'Nice shape' is too simple. Explaining this further would help to demonstrate knowledge and understanding of aesthetics.

SKILL BUILDER 12.2

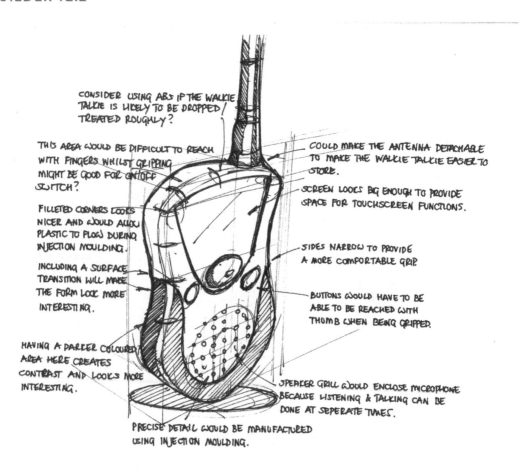

SKILL BUILDER 13.1

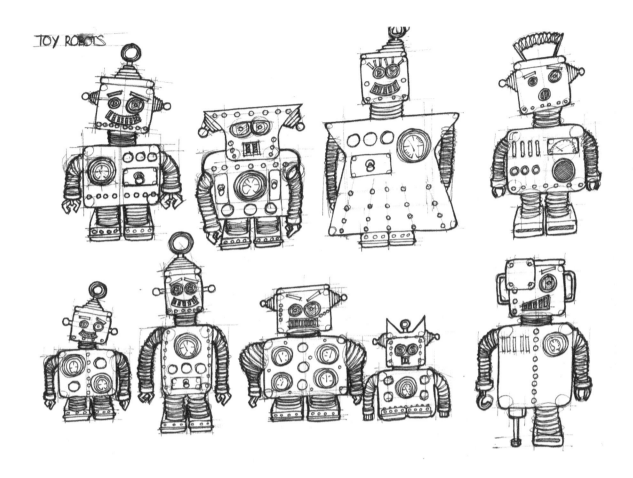

SKILL BUILDER 13.2

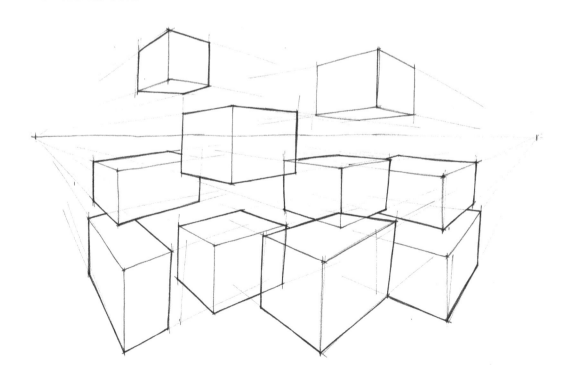

SKILL BUILDER 13.3

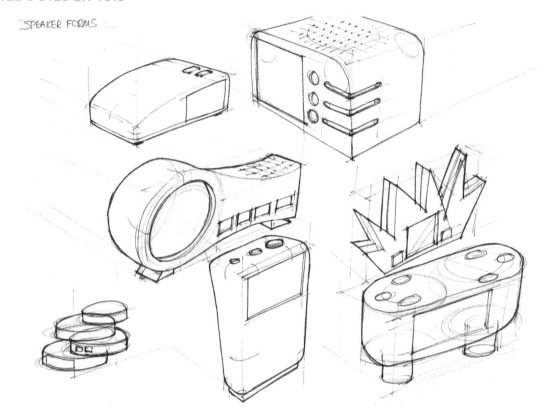

SPEAKER FORMS

SKILL BUILDER 13.4

SKILL BUILDER 14.1

The use of 3D computer models brings many advantages for the manufacturer, these include:

- Reduced storage space during the modelling and development stage, as virtual models can be stored on disk or online. This can be a significant benefit when working on large-scale products.
- Ease of editing – changes to computer-generated models can be made quickly without the need to remake large parts of a physical model.
- 3D computer models can be tested using simulators to see how the product would react under different conditions. This is particularly useful when designing buildings, bridges, aircraft and cars, where consumer safety is paramount.
- 3D models can be fully rendered and used for presenting to the client and in promotional materials for the product.
- Integration of CAD/CAM facilities results in a more streamlined progression from design through to the final manufacture.

The benefits to the manufacturer have a knock-on effect for the consumer, mostly in the areas of safety and cost. Because the development process and the transition between development and manufacture is speeded up, the development costs tend to be reduced. This usually results in a reduced retail price for the consumer. The use of testing and simulation software reduces the number of products that arrive on the market with faults, hopefully resulting in safer products.

SKILL BUILDER 14.2

Advantages

- Rapid prototyping (RP) machines can produce highly complex and detailed parts without the need for moulds.
- Products can be designed or altered quickly to meet the specific requirements of the client or consumer.
- Some RP products can be manufactured as one part, reducing the need for assembly of the product.

Disadvantages

- The actual manufacturing speed is slow, reducing the output potential.
- Currently the number of different materials that can be used during the RP process is relatively low. This limits the types of products that can be manufactured.
- Reduced economy of scale due to the low number of products likely to be manufactured.

SKILL BUILDER 16.1

The most important material requirements for a bottle opener are:

- **Strength**, as the opener will have to exert a force upon the bottle seal (either cork or lid) to remove it.
- **Chemical**, as the bottle opener will have to withstand being washed and having different liquids (potentially corrosive) spilled over it.
- **Stiffness**, as the bottle opener won't be able to lever off metal lids if there is too much flexibility.

The most important material requirements for casing for a hairdryer are:

- **Thermal**, as the casing will have to withstand the high temperatures needed to heat the air to dry the hair.
- **Electrical**, to protect the user from the electrical current used to operate the motor and heating elements in the hairdryer case.
- The materials will have to be **able to be formed** into the fairly complex range of forms hairdryers come in these days.

The most important material requirements for a tennis racket frame are:

- **Weight**, as the racket must be able to be held and swung for long periods of time. This must be the case for a range of users.
- **Stiffness**, as the racket is used to strike a ball sometimes at great pace and with lots of force. There shouldn't be too much force lost to any flaw in the frame.
- **Strength** because, although the racket must be light, it must also withstand the forces generated when the ball is struck.

The most important material requirements for a bicycle frame are:

- **Hardness**, as the frame must withstand scratches and wear and tear.
- **Weight**, as the frame is one of the largest components of the bike it is the one most likely to add to the weight. Weight must be kept down so that the bike is easy to move.
- **Stiffness**, the frame shouldn't flex too much when subjected to the weight of the user. Too much flex in the frame also causes the user to waste energy when pedalling.

SKILL BUILDER 18.1

ALUMIMIUM

Soft, ductile, malleable, conductive of heat and electricity. Good strength-to-weight ratio.

Good corrosion resistance.

Used for electronic casing, vehicle parts, window frames, packaging and containers.

MILD STEEL

Good tensile strength, tough, reasonably malleable, ductile with some elasticity.

Low corrosion resistance – requires protective finishes such as galvanising or painting with oil-based paints.

Used for vehicle bodies, nuts, screws and in girders used for large structures such as bridges and buildings.

HIGH CARBON STEEL

Harder, less ductile and less malleable than mild steel. Tougher than mild steel. Can be hardened and tempered.

Low resistance to corrosion.

Typically used for cutting tools such as drills and chisels.

STAINLESS STEEL

Tough, ductile, higher tensile strength than mild steel.

High resistance to corrosion due to chromium content.

Food safe. Used for many kitchen appliances such as fridges, kettles and toasters. Also used for water taps, sink tops, cutlery, seatbelt, buckles and aircraft components.

ZINC

Soft, ductile and malleable over 100°C. Good corrosion resistance – typically used as a plating (galvanise) on other more corrosive metals.

Used to galvanise items such as fences, roofing and buckets. Alloys used to die cast housings and cast toys.

COPPER

Good heat/electrical conductor, malleable and ductile.

High corrosion resistance.

Used for electrical wiring and components, pricing structures and decorative items such as jewellery and home accessories.

BRASS

Good heat/electrical conductor, harder than copper.

High corrosion resistance although tarnishes easily.

Easily cast. Used for propellers, decorative fixtures and fittings, ornaments and instruments.

BRONZE

Harder and tougher than brass. Hard wearing.

Easily machined.

Good corrosion resistance.

Used for springs, bearings, gears, valves and casting statues.

CAST IRON

Hard, brittle, strong in compression, weak in tension, self lubricating.

Low resistance to corrosion.

Used for machine parts including gear wheels and handles, vices, pans and engine parts.

SKILL BUILDER 22.1

Turning can potentially have a negative environmental impact as it is a subtractive process, so lots of waste material is created (swarf) as the metal part is cut. Cooling fluid needs to be used to prevent the tools or part becoming too hot. This requires energy, generating pollution during the manufacturing stage.

Although waste metal is produced and cooling fluid is used, these can be recycled, decreasing the environmental impact of the process. The metal can be collected and melted down and formed into other components. The fluid can be filtered to remove any swarf and fed back into the cooling system.

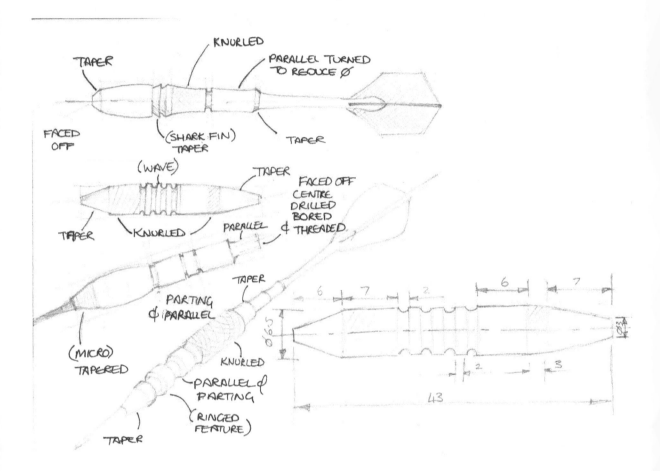

SKILL BUILDER 23.1

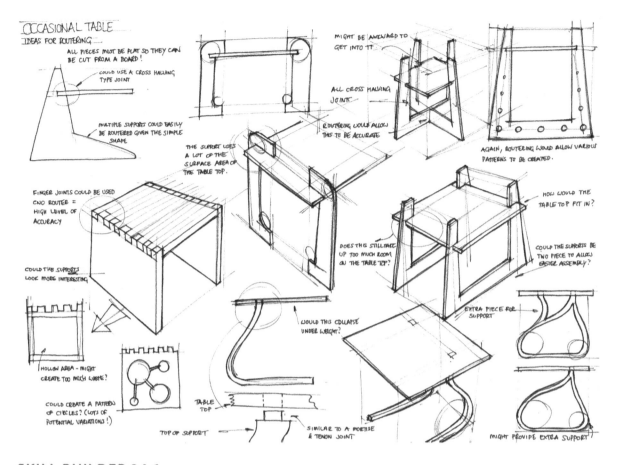

SKILL BUILDER 24.1

1. Sand casting is a suitable manufacturing process as the product does not require a high quality surface finish or dimensional accuracy. The form is simple and could be formed easily with a sand core.

2. Investment casting is suitable for the engine parts as complex parts can be produced with high dimensional accuracy. Also, minimal finishing is required as the wax provides a good quality surface finish.

SKILL BUILDER 25.1

1. Zinc alloy is suitable for die casting the food mixer because it has a high resistance to corrosion, can be used to create thin walls and takes on a good surface finish.

2. Die casting is a suitable process for many of the parts of the food mixer because a high quality surface finish is required. The green housing requires a thin wall and should also incorporate bosses and ribs to aid in the assembly and to strengthen the case. Die casting can incorporate these features with a thin-walled part reducing the overall weight and cost of material used. Die casting also produces parts with the high dimensional accuracy required for parts to fit together and function well. Die casting is also suitable for high volume production runs.

SKILL BUILDER 25.2

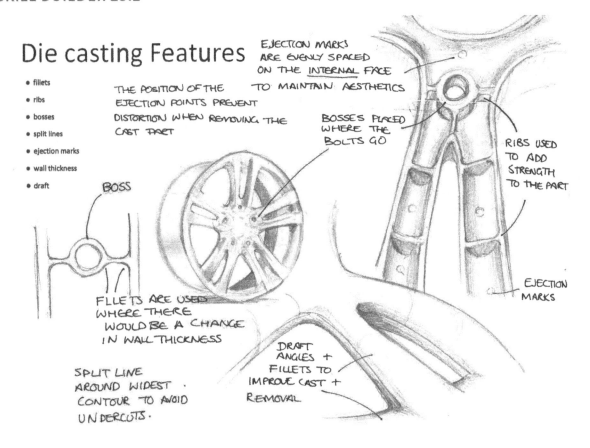

Die casting Features

EJECTION MARKS ARE EVENLY SPACED ON THE INTERNAL FACE TO MAINTAIN AESTHETICS

- fillets
- ribs
- bosses
- split lines
- ejection marks
- wall thickness
- draft

THE POSITION OF THE EJECTION POINTS PREVENT DISTORTION WHEN REMOVING THE CAST PART

BOSSES PLACED WHERE THE BOLTS GO

RIBS USED TO ADD STRENGTH TO THE PART

BOSS

FILLETS ARE USED WHERE THERE WOULD BE A CHANGE IN WALL THICKNESS

EJECTION MARKS

SPLIT LINE AROUND WIDEST CONTOUR TO AVOID UNDERCUTS.

DRAFT ANGLES + FILLETS TO IMPROVE CAST + REMOVAL

SKILL BUILDER 26.1

The simplistic design of these children's chairs lends itself to manufacture from lengths of extruded plastic.

The chair is comprised of two different sections of material: one for the legs and frame, and the other for the backrest and seat. These two basic elements could be extruded as long lengths of two different sections before being cut into shorter lengths for assembling to form the complete chair. The individual lengths of cut material could then simply be screwed or bonded together.

Moulding the individual parts for the chair would be more costly as the tooling costs for injection moulding are much higher than for extrusion.

The most suitable material would be HDPE because this is readily available as a recycled plastic, comes in a range of colours and won't fade in the sunlight or split or chip.

SKILL BUILDER 26.2

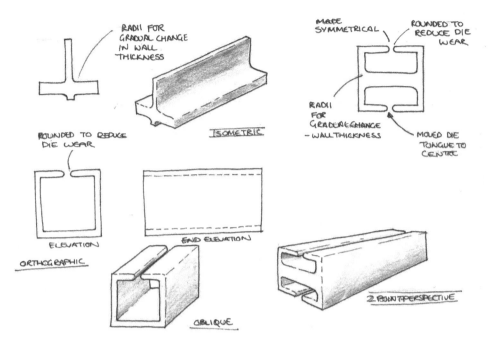

SKILL BUILDER 27.1

1. Drop forging is suitable for manufacturing the G-cramp because the form is simple, there are no thin wall sections and the process strengthens the metal.
2. The hole may have been produced using secondary processes. This may include machining the forged part by boring a hole before threading the internal surface.

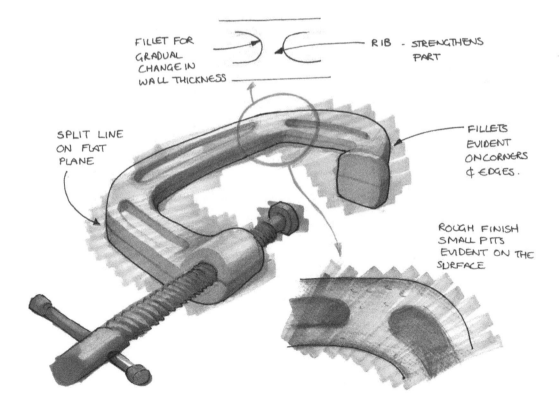

SKILL BUILDER 28.1

The poorly designed calculator case has been refined so that it can be manufactured using injection moulding.

The case should be made from ABS plastic because this material is strong, highly durable and lightweight. It is also scratch resistant, so the calculator is less likely to show signs of wear.

The folio page below shows how the case has been refined to allow it to be successfully manufactured using injection moulding.

The following refinements have been made:

- The sides have been angled to allow the case to be removed easily from the mould.
- Bosses have been added to allow the case to be screwed together. These bosses are tapered, again to allow easy removal from the mould.
- Where bosses have been added these are supported using webs that connect the bosses to the side wall.
- The edges and internal corners have been rounded to reduce the likelihood of the edges chipping and the internal corners cracking.

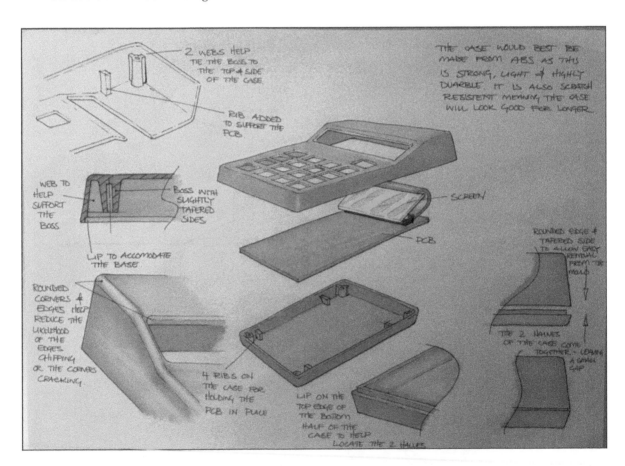

SKILL BUILDER 29.1

The novelty rubber door wedge shown below was manufactured using the process of compression moulding. We can tell this because of the noticeable draft angle on the vertical surfaces and the high-quality finish on the top surface.

Compression moulding has been chosen over injection moulding for the manufacture of the door wedge because of the simplistic form and lack of undercuts in the product.

The choice of material, silicon rubber, also lends itself towards compression moulding. Injection moulding silicon rubber is more complicated than using other plastics and requires specific moulding machines.

Injection moulding could have been used to produce the wedge but the cost of the moulds needed and alterations to the moulding machine would have greatly increased the overall cost of the product. The number of products likely to be sold also lends itself to compression moulding, which is more suited to low-volume production runs.

SKILL BUILDER 30.1

The shampoo bottle shown on page 165 has been refined so that it can be manufactured using injection blow moulding.

It was decided that the container should be made from LDPE plastic because this material is tough, flexible and resistant to chemicals.

The folio page below shows how the bottle has been refined to allow it to be successfully manufactured using injection blow moulding.

The following refinements have been made:

- The bottle is symmetrical, with the split line for the mould running along the line of symmetry.
- The sides have been tapered, creating a draft, to allow the bottle to be removed easily from the mould.
- The edges have also been rounded to allow the plastic to reach the full extents of the mould, reducing the risk of the bottle getting stuck in the mould.
- The sprue pin has been positioned at the base of the bottle and some additional detailing added, to allow the bottle to sit flat and not wobble.
- The level of detail required for the threaded spout has been considered and further testing of the wall thickness is required.

The cap for the bottle could not be blow moulded, due to the level of detail and fine tolerance of the thread. Because of this, it was decided to manufacture the cap using injection moulding.

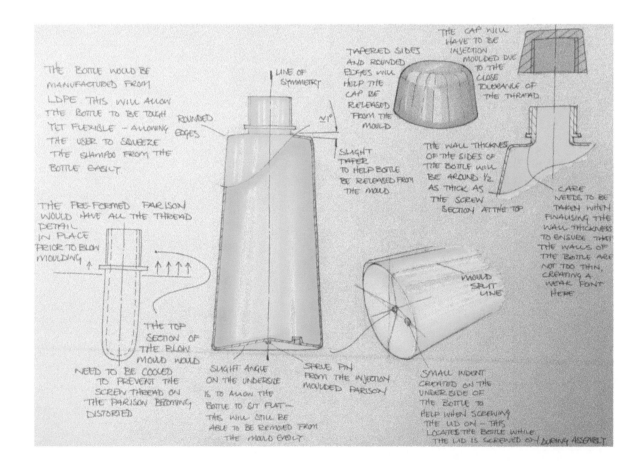

SKILL BUILDER 31.1

The oil container shown on page 167 has been refined so that it can be manufactured using extrusion blow moulding.

It was decided that the container should be made from HDPE plastic because this material is strong, highly durable and resistant to chemicals.

The folio page below shows how the container has been refined to allow it to be successfully manufactured using extrusion blow moulding.

The following refinements have been made:

- The sides have been tapered to allow the container to be removed easily from the mould.
- The edges have also been rounded to allow the plastic to reach the full extents of the mould, reducing the risk of the container getting stuck in the mould.
- The level of detail required around the spout has been kept to a minimum to allow the container to be extrusion blow moulded.
- The container is symmetrical, with the split line for the mould running along the line of symmetry.

The level of detail and thread on the cap for the container meant it could not be blow moulded. Because of this, it was decided to manufacture the cap using compression moulding.

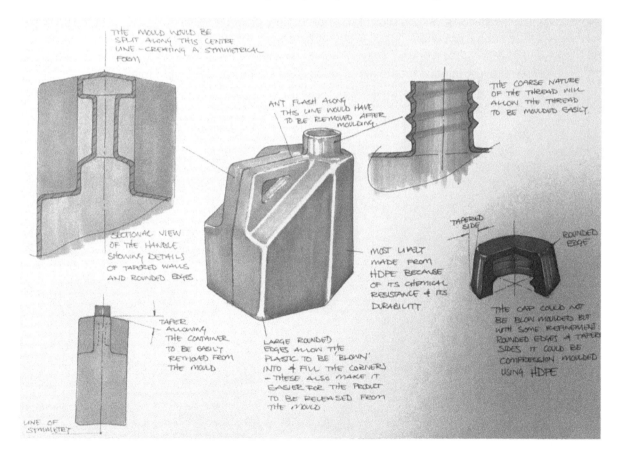

SKILL BUILDER 32.1

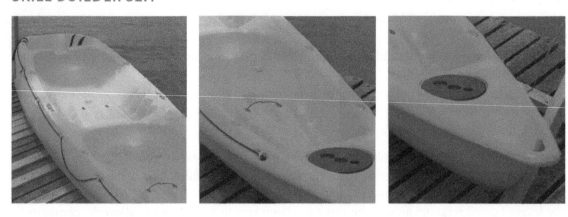

The kayak was probably manufactured using rotational moulding and there are a number of visual features that allow the process to be identified.

- The detailing on the top of the kayak is tapered inwards towards the bottom of the boat, allowing it to be easily removed from the mould at the end of the moulding cycle.
- The hollow form could only have been achieved using rotational moulding or blow moulding, but the form of the kayak is too complex to have been blow moulded. Also the detailing at the tip of the kayak could not have been produced using blow moulding.
- The mixing of the red and yellow colours in a random pattern is created by adding different colours of polyester powder into the mould and allowing them to mix as the mould rotates.

SKILL BUILDER 33.1

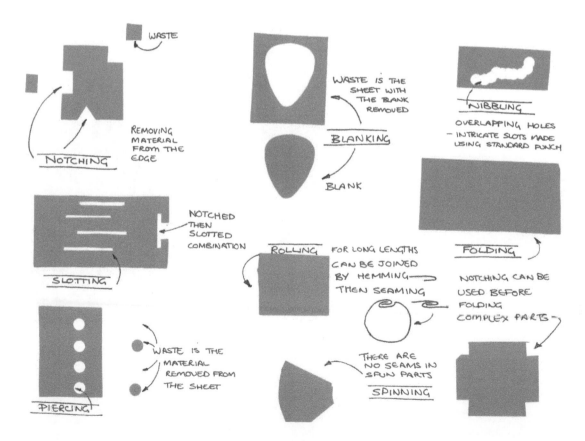

SKILL BUILDER 35.1

The packaging for the potato peeler shown on page 175 has been designed so that it can be manufactured using vacuum forming.

It was decided that the packaging should be made in two parts. The backing sheet will be made from stiff card and have all the details required for sale preprinted on it. The card will then be stapled to a vacuum-formed shell made from PET.

PET was selected because it is clear (easy to see through), allowing the sales details to be read, and it is also commonly used in the food industry as it is hygienic.

The folio page below shows details of the design of the packaging.

The following features have been incorporated:

1. The sides have been angled to allow the shell to be easily removed from the pattern.

2. The edges and corners have been rounded to reduce the likelihood of the PET over-stretching and thinning as it is formed across the edges.

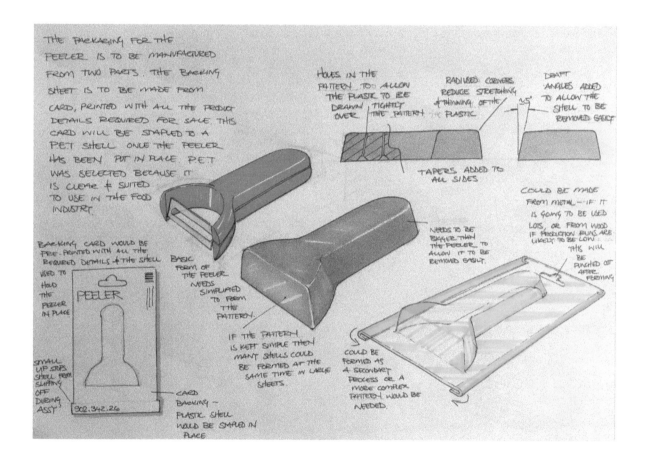

SKILL BUILDER 36.1

Tanglewood Guitar Tuner

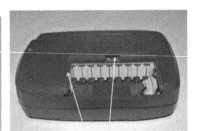

The tuner casing is made up from two main parts. The design is very simple in terms of the number of individual parts. This means only a few joining methods are needed. This helps to keep manufacturing costs down.

A separate battery cover slides into the casing and is secured using a clip designed into the plastic. Designing the joining method into the plastic negates the need for extra components to be made or purchased.

You can see the grooves that the battery cover slides into and the hole left for the clip in this image. Using the two methods together, provide a tight and secure fit for the cover.

Two small screws are used to join the sides of the casing. You can see the bosses that they are screwed into here.

Using screws has multiple advantages. The case can be disassembled if it stops working. As they are standard components, screws can be easily sourced and replaced if they go missing.

The most likely reason they are used here is cost. When purchased in massive bulk they will be very inexpensive. It is probably cheaper to design and manufacture the fittings for screws to go into than to add the detail to the die for injection moulding required to use plastic clips all the way around.

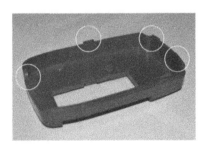

Plastic guides provide extra security around the perimeter of the casing. The screws hold the case together centrally and these plastic guides prevent any further movement. These are designed as a part of the case and reduce the need for any more than two screws to be used.

The plastic guides are located in these gaps in the opposite of the casing. Again, this provides extra security in the fit without the need for further components or fixings.

Soldering is used extensively in wiring of the printed circuit board. Solder provides a strong enough fixing and connection that will also conduct electrical current.

SKILL BUILDER 36.2

MIG An electric arc forms between a consumable wire electrode and the work pieces. The work pieces melt from the heat of the arc and are joined together with added filler metal from the wire.

Metal Inert Gas Welding   Can be automatic or semi-automatic

Advantages

- No slag to chip
- Can be used on thin materials
- High production rate
- Portable
- Little practice required, easy to learn
- Electrodes not specific to material thickness

Disadvantages

- Requires a wire feeder
- Less portable due to wire feeder
- Difficult to get the gun in small spaces
- Can't be used in the wind as inert gas is required

TIG This is a manual or semi-automatic welding process that uses a non-consumable tungsten electrode to produce an electric arc.

Tungsten Inert Gas Welding   TIG is commonly used to weld thin sections of stainless steel, aluminium, magnesium and copper alloys.

Advantages

- Achieves the highest quality welds of all the ARC welding processes
- Good quality surface finish
- Can be used for fine work, including dentistry
- Can be used in conjunction with MIG
- Can weld dissimilar metals
- Can weld materials from 0.5mm
- Argon gas can be used to weld all materials
- Can be used without filler wire

Disadvantages

- Time-slower than MIG
- Correct electrodes must be used
- Requires the operator to use both hands (torch and filler wire)
- Requires a high degree of skill from the operator

SPOT Welding

This involves holding sheets of metal together with two copper alloy electrodes. A current causes the metals to fuse.

Often selected for joining sheet metal fabrications and assemblies because it is fast, reliable and economical.

Advantages

- Usually free from burn and splash
- Quality of weld not dependent on ability/skill of worker
- Easy to control
- Low material cost
- Easy clean up
- Fast

Disadvantages

- Requires space
- Weaker than other welds
- Porous
- Limited to 12" thickness due to current

SMAW — Shielded Metal Arc Welding

Oldest and most versatile of the welding processes. It is a manual process that uses a consumable metal electrode coated in flux to create the weld. An electric current from a welding power supply is used to create an electric arc between the electrode and the metals to be joined.

One of the most commonly used processes in the maintenance and repair industry.

Advantages

- Low equipment cost. No bottle, gas hose, flowmeter, or tig rig/wire feeder needed
- Quick change from one material to another
- Can be used in confined spaces
- Portable
- Special electrodes are available for cutting/gouging
- Requires no outside shielding gas
- Can be used outdoors in mild winds

Disadvantages

- Filler metal cost per weld can be greater due to a low deposition efficiency that can vary greatly with stub length
- Slower production rate due to rod changes
- Needs good hand–eye coordination
- Slag must be removed

SKILL BUILDER 38.1

Answers to the questions on page 184.

1. Task 5 (9 weeks)

2. Week 10 sees the workforce working on four different tasks at the same time

3. Task 1 (week 1), Task 2 (week 5), Task 8 (weeks 17 and 18), Task 9 (weeks 19 and 20) and Task 10 (weeks 22–24)

4. Two, tasks 5 and 7

5. 15 weeks

6. 46 weeks to complete the project sequentially minus the 24 weeks on the chart = 22 additional weeks

SKILL BUILDER 38.2

The complete flowchart detailing the steps required to make buttered toast is shown below.

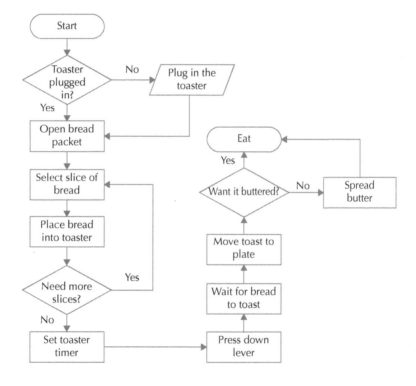

SKILL BUILDER 38.3

Cue cards detailing line, cell and just-in-time (JIT) manufacturing setups.

Line production

Highly specialised production lines are designed to output large volumes of the same product. These lines are often highly automated and require high initial setup costs. The process does not have to be stopped and restarted for each new product.

Advantages:
- Can output high volumes of the same product very quickly.
- Economies of scale decrease the unit cost.

Disadvantages:
- Inflexibility; products have to be very similar or standardised and cannot be tailored to individual tastes.
- Line production systems can be pretty boring for employees to operate. Staff motivation is an important issue for management to consider.
- High initial setup costs.

Cell production

Highly flexible production cells that are used to produce a range of similar product types. These cells are manned by teams of skilled operators, capable of completing each of the tasks within the cell. The cells can be quickly altered to produce different products.

Advantages:
- Employee tasks are changed throughout the day, helping maintain employee motivation.
- Flexibility allows for a larger product range to be manufactured.
- Can react quickly to changes in the market with minimal costs.

Disadvantages:
- High initial setup costs.
- Not suitable for large volumes.

Just-in-Time (JIT) production

Used as a stock control mechanism, often as part of line and cell production systems. JIT increases efficiency and reduces waste by having materials and subcontracted parts delivered to the factory when they are needed.

Advantages:
- Reduced storage space for stock.
- Inventory costs are reduced because large volumes of materials are not held in stock.

Disadvantages:
- Requires accurate projections of product demand; getting this wrong can have costly consequences.
- Requires good delivery networks (rail and road) between suppliers and the factory.
- Relies on computerised stock control system.
- Risks of supplier defaulting and not being able to meet the terms of the contract.

SKILL BUILDER 38.4

The use of CNC production brings many benefits to the consumer.

- Because flat-packed product parts are manufactured more accurately by CNC, they tend to fit together more easily at the home assembly stage, resulting in increased customer satisfaction.
- Final retail costs of products have become lower as a result of CNC manufacture. This is largely due to the retailer passing on any savings from reduced manufacturing costs.
- Finally, an increasing number of retailers are selling products in the form of the CNC file. This allows consumers to manufacture the product and assemble it themselves. They are also able to make alterations to the original file, tailoring the product to their specific needs. This form of retail relies on the consumer having access to CNC machines, but is revolutionising the way products are being purchased and manufactured.

SKILL BUILDER 38.5

The use of CAD/CAM greatly reduces the number of skilled tradespeople within an engineering workshop because a number of CNC machines can be operated by one person, resulting in job losses in some cases.

Because the use of CNC machinery allows highly complex parts to be made with very little human input, the need for skilled pattern makers and tool makers has greatly reduced.

Skill levels within workshops are reduced as a result of automated machining; highly skilled tradespeople have been replaced with semi-skilled CNC operators, whose job it is to clear any faults and keep the machines running.

SKILL BUILDER 39.1

Select a readily available product and use the questions associated with the 6Rs to help establish a starting point for the redesign of the product.

Rethink – Is there actually a need for the selfie stick?
The current trend for taking 'selfie'-style photos has generated a desire from the consumer for this type of product, but not a need. This is the case with many modern consumer-driven products; companies have shifted from focusing on what the consumer needs to focusing more on what they want.

Refuse – What impact does the manufacture have on the environment?
The product seems to be made of five commonly used materials (brass, steel, EVA foam, polypropylene and polyurethane rubber), the production of which does not have major impacts on the environment. The primary manufacturing process used in the production is injection moulding, and again this is not viewed as having a major impact on the environment. The distance between the manufacture and point of sale can have an impact on the environment and the distance between these should be considered when deciding on where products are manufactured or materials sourced.

Reduce – Could the selfie stick be manufactured using less material or energy?
The product is simplistic in form and looks like the amount of material used and number of manufacturing methods have been kept to a minimum.

Reuse – Can the selfie stick, or parts of it, be used to make another product?
Very few parts can be reused to any great effect. The phone clamp (shown) can be removed and used to mount a phone on to a camera tripod, should the rest of the product break. The main body of the stick (the top of which is also shown) could also be used in conjunction with any camera with a tripod-mount fitting.

Repair – Has the selfie stick been designed in a way that allows for repair?
The selfie stick has not been designed with repair in mind, since the methods of fixing individual parts together are permanent.

Recycle – How easily can the selfie stick be recycled?
The selfie stick will be difficult to recycle due to the number of different materials used and the ways in which they are joined together. Different materials have been moulded in situ and cannot be separated to allow them to be properly recycled. The materials are not easily identifiable by most consumers.

Starting point for the new design
The following points could be considered in redesigning the product:

- Strive to source materials close to the manufacturing plant and the point of sale.
- Where possible, try to design the new product in such a way as to allow parts of the product to be recyclable at the end of its lifecycle.
- Look for ways to make the product easier to repair.
- Look for ways to make the product easier to recycle – use fewer permanent fixings and make materials more easily identifiable.
- Continue to manufacture the selfie stick from as few different materials as possible.

SKILL BUILDER 39.2

The mind map below identifies the issues associated with the illegal mining of tin in the developing world.

Some of the areas of conflict between the producers and the consumers are as follows:

- Tin mining provides a valuable source of income for local communities, with families often relying on this money to provide food, shelter and education. However, to meet demand for tin, children are often involved in mining, frequently in dangerous and unregulated conditions. These issues cause concern for some consumers due to our views on the exploitation of children in the workplace and because we expect our workplaces to implement strict health and safety standards.

- Mining causes the destruction of the local environment, which is largely overlooked by the local community as the need to earn money is paramount. Consumers in the developed world have become more aware of the need to preserve the natural environment, resulting in further conflicting views.

- The need for tin is largely created through consumers' desire for newer, more technologically advanced products, most of which will never be owned by the people who produce the raw materials. Is it fair that the producers of the product will never have the income to own the product?

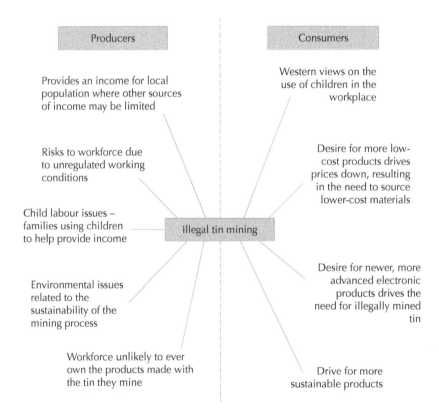

SKILL BUILDER 39.3

The 6R's (below) have been used as a starting point to help identify conflicts between environmental, economic, social and cultural beliefs associated with the manufacture and distribution of the hoodie.

Rethink – Is there actually a need for the low-cost hoodie?

Refuse – What impact does its manufacture have on the environment?

Reduce – Has the hoodie been manufactured using the least amount of material and energy?

Reuse – Can the hoodie, or parts of it, be used to make another product?

Repair – Has the hoodie been designed in a way that allows for repair?

Recycle – How easily can the hoodie be recycled?

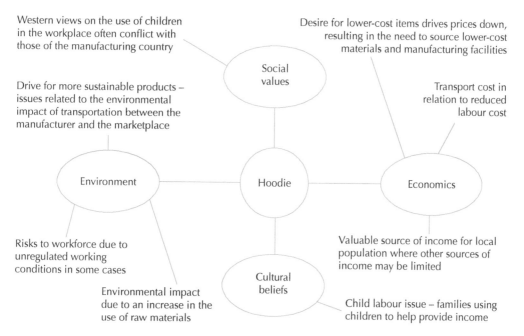

The mind map shows some of the issues of conflict associated with the manufacture and distribution of the hoodie.

Today's economic climate dictates that there is a need for low-cost clothing, much of which is produced in the developing world and shipped to the marketplace in the developed world. Tackling the issues below would go a long way to resolving some of the conflict.

- Regulation of workplaces to ensure safe working conditions for all of those involved in the manufacture. It is unlikely that pressure from the developed world would be able to remove children from the workplace, but making the workplace safer would go a long way to help ease the concerns of the those in the developed world.

- The shipping costs in relation to the environmental impact of shipping needs to be considered carefully. However, encouraging manufacture to take place closer to the marketplace would have an impact on the number of jobs in the developing world.

- Providing a fair wage for those who make the garments needs to be considered and the use of Fairtrade-type organisations should be encouraged.